T0348136

BWB Texts

Short books on big subjects from great New Zealand writers

Imagining
Decolonisation

First published in 2020 by Bridget Williams Books Ltd, PO Box 12474,
Wellington 6144, New Zealand, www.bwb.co.nz, info@bwb.co.nz.

Reprinted 2020 (twice), 2021 (twice), 2022 (twice) and 2023.

ISBN 9781988545783 (Paperback), ISBN 9781988545752 (EPUB)
ISBN 9781988545769 (Kindle), ISBN 9781988545776 (PDF)
DOI https://doi.org/10.7810/9781988545783

A catalogue record for this book is available from the National Library of
New Zealand. Kei te pātengi raraunga o Te Puna Mātauranga o Aotearoa te
whakarārangi o tēnei pukapuka.

Acknowledgements
The publisher acknowledges the ongoing support provided by the Bridget
Williams Books Publishing Trust. The commitment of Creative New Zealand
to good New Zealand publishing is also acknowledged, and its support for this
publication is appreciated.

Publisher: Tom Rennie
Editor: Anna Hodge
Cover and internal design: Neil Pardington Design
Typesetter: Tina Delceg
Printer: Blue Star, Wellington

CONTENTS

INTRODUCTION

BIANCA ELKINGTON
(NGĀTI TOA RANGATIRA) AND
JENNIE SMEATON
(NGĀTI TOA RANGATIRA)

In 2017 we were working on a project about decolonisation and our urban spaces, using Porirua as a case study. Led by Jasmine Arthur from Ngāti Toa, we took a bus tour around the area with some high school students from many different cultures and ethnic backgrounds, seeking to understand the local history and some of the processes that had shaped the city. At the base of Battle Hill, we stopped to talk to the students about decolonisation and what it might look like.

'But what is colonisation?' one student asked. We talked about the basics – the ways that Pākehā ideas about society and land and relationships were imposed on Māori, how Ngāti Toa land was taken by the state without compensation, how most of the land has never been returned, and how Ngāti Toa has had to pay for some of the land it *has* gotten back.

The student, really annoyed by this point, said, 'But who said they could do that?!'

As soon as the students understood what colonisation was and is – the forceful taking of land, language, culture and autonomy without permission, without anyone 'saying that they could'; the imposition of one group's will on another – they wanted to think about ways the situation could be addressed and redressed. This book is for those students and other people like them who want to know how we got here, and what we can do next.

To understand the desire for decolonisation, we need to understand the diverse ways that colonisation has impacted on Māori. We tell two personal stories below.

BIANCA

When I was the age of the students with us on the bus tour, the term 'colonisation' had no connection to my reality – or so I thought. However, if someone had shown me a movie of my younger years and titled certain scenes 'colonial influence', the links would have been clear.

My life revolved around playing with cousins until late, sleeping at their homes, eating at their tables, being disciplined by anyone who was related to my mum, playing on and around our marae, Takapūwāhia – being Māori was inherent and natural. I never needed to define who I was to others, and certainly never felt that our way of life was different to the norm. The way we lived, with whānau at the centre of our world and manaakitanga an important part of our make-up, had been passed on from generation to generation, and although the landscape around us changed, our sense of belonging remained.

Takapūwāhia was a haven for us – a place where we felt safe, where we belonged and where others saw our potential and shared that with us. Our dreams were everyone's dreams. Our whakapapa connected us, and although as children we didn't know the exact links, we knew we were whānau and that was enough. My educational experience, however, provides a backdrop to understanding the effects colonisation had on me and many other Māori trying to navigate their way through two worlds.

Primary education was local: the school was an extension of our community and we all felt it. We walked to school together, and when one of us was away for a tangi or other whānau event, we were all away. It wasn't uncommon to see our teachers and principal at the marae for tangi, a blessing of a baby or a significant birthday. These years were the best years I had in school.

But then there came a point in my education where going to school outside of our area was necessary. Our mum, a recent widow, was enrolled at teachers' training college and felt we would benefit if we attended the more privileged schools outside of our community. I found myself outside Porirua, in a Pākehā school system in a predominantly Pākehā community, in search of a 'quality' education. I quickly realised there were aspects of my reality I had to leave behind in order to stay out of the spotlight.

Successful integration into the new school community required a certain amount of sacrifice of my own cultural norms. I needed to learn new norms quickly, or stay out of sight. To be invisible, there were parts of my life I felt I needed to hide – parts that didn't fit with the majority. I didn't want people knowing that most times when I wasn't at school it was because I was at a tangi. That wasn't 'normal'. Some of my Pākehā friends had never been to a funeral, they told me. I didn't want people to know that sometimes I had dinner at my auntie's, that my cousins would come over all the time, or that my mother was one of thirteen children. Those things made me different from the norm, and being different didn't feel like a safe thing.

At this high school I had a Pākehā teacher who never handed me maths homework. Eventually I built up the courage to ask her why she skipped me every week.

'Your people don't do it anyway', she responded.

'Who do you mean when you say "your people"?'

Her retort was loud: 'Māori.'

In that moment I realised that not everyone expected the best from me. I was now a member of a minority, and school became a game of survival. The teacher confirmed to me that yes, I did have to be someone else to survive in this game. My constant recollection of this experience and inevitable dislike of maths led me to the field of education. I planned to become a teacher, for many different reasons. I wanted to contribute to young people's lives through teaching, but I also knew that I needed to know the language of this colonial game so that I could help other whānau, Māori whānau in my community, have a positive educational experience. The Pākehā education system disregarded our culture; it disregarded our belief systems. I wanted whānau to experience learning that was embedded in who we are. Twenty years later, that seed grew into the iwi-based educational programme Te Puna Mātauranga.

Te Puna Mātauranga is a hub for education. Nestled in the heart of Takapūwāhia, it provides one-to-one support for primary and secondary students and access to information and support for whānau. Te Puna Mātauranga has acted as the voice of many whānau as they come across challenges in schools. A small group of passionate iwi educators continues to provide support and resources to many students and whānau within the community.

My whānau have felt land injustices at first hand. As a child, I grew up knowing that the Public Works Act had directly affected our whānau and whenua.[1] I remember many years ago attending a hui as a young child in our nan's house with an emerging Māori lawyer, to talk about the different options for beginning the process of reclaiming our whenua. I heard stories of how our land had been used by my koro and his children, and how, although the government of the day had supposedly taken it for state housing, it was never used by them for that purpose but was also never given back.

My auntie fought for more than twenty years and finally, just before she passed away, the land was offered back to our whānau, for a price – despite the method of government acquisition. We paid that price, and now have our land back, on which we will build a papakāinga for our whānau. This story of losing and regaining whenua is not just our story, but the story of many Māori whānau around the country.

The story highlights the intentions the government of the day had to redefine Māori and Pākehā relations. However, colonial influence continues to be felt via systems and legislation that are meant to help and empower Māori through the return of their land. There is much work to do, but when we *know* more we *do* more. That *knowing* to me is an act of decolonisation.

JENNIE

We come from a community where our whānau still live near to one another. Our marae, Takapūwāhia, is at the heart of this community. Our papakāinga is located less than 200 metres from the harbour's edge and close to the heart of Porirua.

One of my earliest memories is of when my auntie told me to jump into the harbour, Te Awarua o Porirua. Like all kids standing on the end of the jetty, I jumped. What a heck of a surprise we all got! That was my first close-up encounter with the feeling of fine silty sediment created from pollutants of various types caused by land reclamation and urban development. What a disappointment this was as kids wanting to swim and play in this awa of such significance to our iwi. Links to the natural world run deep in our community.

One group of our uncles is known as the 'E TU boys' (uncles held in high regard). They get together every Sunday and do service work around Takapūwāhia, including the maintenance and upkeep of our urupā and marae grounds. Once upon a time, for one week of the year, these uncles would go and camp by the harbour. They'd set up for the whole week on Wineera Drive, by the harbour's edge. They'd put the fishing net down for a week, trying to do the activities that had been done for decades before them. I'm not even sure if they ate the fish or if it was too paru but that wasn't the point. For them it was about reconnecting with the awa, and doing what they had once done, by sharing memories, stories and simply dropping the net and pulling it back in.

We at Takapūwāhia – or 'the Pā' as we call it – have had a city build itself around us. We've been urbanised only reluctantly. In some respects, the process has been good, and in some not so good. It's meant we have had to adapt and we continue to do so.

We live with the stories from kaumātua of a time gone by: of being baptised, fishing, feeding our manuhiri, all in or from our awa. But our generation has never been able to physically connect with the harbour like our kaumātua once did. It has been polluted for as long as I've been alive.

When I think of the journeys that our iwi has been on through successive generations, it's been a constant fight. The fight continues today, I guess – it's just over different kaupapa, more reflective of the time we are in. Nonetheless, it's a fight to preserve who we are and the way we live. We want the best community to live in, and one where our grandchildren can play. Our world is our community and we love it. Everything we do is to make a better place for our whānau.

I fell into the environmental space by accident. I had come to work for Ngāti Toa in my late twenties to do communications, but over a period of time it became apparent to me that I actually wanted to be working in environmental management. I had great mentors: Tā Matiu Rei, Miria Pomare, Graeme Hastilow, Dr Taku Parai, our kaumātua and many more outside the iwi. Our role as Ngāti Toa was to influence what was happening in our community and wider rohe. We needed to be active and present to influence policy and decision-makers in order to get better environmental outcomes, inclusive of a Māori worldview. The mahi in this space never stops; our taiao needs us to be constantly active and vigilant. We hope one day to get to a point where our awa will once again nourish our whānau with the pipi and cockles of days gone by.

Due to the fact that the creek has been piped, whenever it rains there is nowhere for the water to go and the roads channel it towards houses and the marae. These seemingly small but impactful acts of colonisation continue to affect our iwi. I look forward to the day when our homes will be protected from heavy rain events, when we can put away our sandbags without fear of flood, and when our wharenui, Toa Rangatira, is protected from stormwater breaches. Then maybe some of the stories that we listen to from my whānau, about the activities we used to do on the land and the harbour, might one day become a reality.

At the bottom of Te Hiko Street in Takapūwāhia, there's a bus stop painted by a Ngāti Toa artist inspired by the thoughts and ideas of tamariki. It depicts manu aute, people doing mahi on the beach and other daily activities on the papakāinga. The tamariki could have suggested painting jet skis, or other modern things, but they chose to depict us, as Māori, undertaking our traditional practices. What a beautiful thought to have: our tamariki re-Indigenising and restoring our landscape. It is awesome.

WHAT THIS BOOK IS ABOUT

This book is for all New Zealanders exploring what decolonisation looks like; how we can all contribute to it, irrespective of whether we're Māori or not; and why we might want to. It is not the definitive book on decolonisation – others have more expertise to write such a book than we do. We want here to speak simply about what we think it means for our society. All of us except Amanda have Māori whakapapa, and we each draw on our own stories and differing experiences of colonisation to discuss something that should be important to everyone. Pākehā allied voices such as Amanda's are important as decolonisation is the work of all of us, despite the need for decolonising efforts to be led by Māori. Every New Zealander needs to know about colonisation and its impacts. After coming to grips with these colonising effects, we want to demystify the idea of decolonisation and show that

16

it is something that every New Zealander can get on board with and benefit from.

The idea for the book grew out of a project we were involved in, Imagining Decolonised Cities, a collaboration between Te Puna Mātauranga, Ngāti Toa Rangatira and Victoria University of Wellington.[2] We wanted to think about decolonisation and what it might mean for our towns and cities, and we chose to focus on Porirua – the whenua of Ngāti Toa Rangatira; Bianca and Jennie's tūrangawaewae.

The first phase of the project involved working with high school students from Porirua. When we started preparing for the wānanga with these rangatahi, it became clear that there wasn't really much available that was written in an accessible way to help explain colonisation and decolonisation to rangatahi and adults alike. Imagining Decolonised Cities was all about engaging both Māori and non-Māori to think about – to imagine – what a decolonised city might look and feel like. We knew we needed Pākehā and other non-Māori to be thinking about these questions as well as Māori if we are ever going to move forward towards decolonisation. How could we do that if we couldn't explain it? This book is our response: an effort to explore the impact of colonisation on Māori *and* non-Māori, and to work out what it might mean to decolonise our systems and spaces to create a more just society.

Colonisation and decolonisation are hairy terms, however. Both can seem politically loaded and fear-inducing. A broad definition of colonisation is that it's a process of one group imposing their ideas about the world on another group, taking away the things that make life possible and good; and that decolonisation is the process of removing those impositions.

Similarly, the term 'Pākehā' has received a lot of flak over the years, and some assume its meaning is derogatory. Most te reo Māori commentators, however, assert that it is not, and that Māori originally used the word to reference mythical beings resembling men that were pale in colour.[3] Throughout this book we use 'Pākehā' to mean non-Māori New Zealanders of European ancestry. We've distinguished between Pākehā and other non-Māori to reflect the fact that most of the dominant systems and institutions in this country are based on ideas from Europe (sometimes called Eurocentric ideas). It's these structures that we think need to change to reflect *this* place, and the people of this place.

Language is another structural thing that underlies life in this place. We use many terms in te reo Māori in this book – sometimes we will stop to explain these, for those who do not speak the reo, but sometimes we won't. If you do not know the meaning of these kupu, we encourage you to look them up in a Māori dictionary as you go.[4]

We have structured the book to try to lead you through key ideas so that, by the end, you will have a clear idea about what decolonisation is and how we might work towards it. In Chapter 1, Mike Ross gives an account of colonisation and explains how the Māori house – the whare – was gradually replaced by a British version. Ocean Ripeka Mercier in Chapter 2 unpacks different forms of decolonisation that have been applied around the world and explains the specific model, underpinned by whakapapa and Kaupapa Māori, that we think might work best in Aotearoa New Zealand. She also warns of the many pitfalls of which aspiring decolonisers should beware. Chapters 3 and 4 by Rebecca Kiddle and Amanda Thomas deal with the impact of colonisation on Pākehā and other non-Māori New Zealanders, explaining that the ill-effects of colonisation reach everyone and providing some practical ideas of how Pākehā can start doing the work of decolonisation. Finally, in Chapter 5, Moana Jackson traces the stories Māori found in this land of Aotearoa that remain strong despite the efforts of colonisation to suppress and co-opt them. It is these stories, he tells us, that can lead us through the process of decolonisation towards a restoration of the way things ought to be – towards a restored future, constantly imagined and reimagined.

Alongside research other people have done, we

include in the chapters that follow some of our own experiences and those of our whānau, to bring to life the thinking and theorising. We hope that this book will be picked up and read by many different people, and that it is useful for thinking about how this country was, is and could be.

1. THE THROAT OF PARATA

MIKE ROSS (NGĀTI HAUĀ)

In Māori tradition, Parata was believed to be a huge creature that lived in the deepest part of the ocean, beyond the horizon, between Aotearoa and foreign lands. Parata was the final destination of all flowing water and it controlled the tides by inhaling and exhaling the ocean's waters. If a voyaging canoe was caught in a great whirlpool or maelstrom and in a place of imminent danger, it was said to be in the mouth or throat of Parata. Ancestors travelling on the Te Arawa canoe found themselves in this exact position. They were saved from certain death only by the powerful incantations of their priest Ngātoroirangi. 'Te waha o te Parata' became a figure of speech describing a person or people unexpectedly falling into a perilous situation. In some ways, the term reflects the experience of colonisation for Māori. Like the unpredictability of the weather and its impact on travelling the oceans, the whirlpool of colonisation and its impacts were an unexpected threat to the survival of Aotearoa and its people.

Colonisation was a brutal process and its effects on Māori have been devastating. However, most New Zealanders are unaware, ignorant or dismissive of how and why colonisation happened and continues to happen, and its effects on society today. In a country that prides itself on giving everyone a fair go, it might be surprising that brutality and apathy remains. Examples of this brutality just from the first half of 2019, if you need some convincing, include many lowlights: a disproportionate number of Māori children living in poverty; consequent pressure on these underprivileged families that can lead to children being removed by an all-powerful state;[1] and continuing racism, like the recent distribution of anti-Māori pamphlets to 'incite negative attitudes towards Māori using misinformation and out of context statements'.[2]

The decolonisation discussed in this book comes out of a complex social and historical story of colonisation. This chapter surveys how theories of colonisation played out in practice in the relationships between Māori and settlers in Aotearoa. Colonisation happens at both a macro and micro level, so brief references are made to historical figures and events. As someone from Ngāti Hauā in the Waikato, I draw on some of my own people's stories that mirror what was happening nationally.

In the conclusion to this chapter, I discuss the fact that, despite the passage of time, a number of Pākehā still believe that the best thing for Māori is to assimilate into the 'mainstream' and reap the benefits of a Pākehā New Zealand. I argue that despite this pressure on Māori to conform to colonial institutions and the ways and values that underpin them, Māori continue with a desire to be Māori – a desire that will drive the project of decolonisation imagined in the chapters to come.[3]

TWO HOUSES

Moana Jackson has described colonisation as the process of replacing one house with another.[4] The houses represent societies and each house provides a secure shelter for the people who live in that house. The strength of a house rests on its foundations; the foundations keep the structure above it sturdy and upright. The foundations of a society include a resource base utilised to ensure its physical survival; a political system to organise it; justice and laws for the security and safety of its citizens; education to maintain and develop it; health practices to support the well-being of its members; and a language to carry its values, views and norms.

Each society has a house with similar foundations but each is organised differently, based on the people's specific beliefs, history, environment and resources. Each house is adorned with its own art traditions, etiquette, myths, stories and music. Each home was built by its owners over centuries of change and improvement. Dynamic political, legal, social and cultural structures evolve over time and iteratively, refined by changing social, political and cultural environments and the knowledge available to its members at any given time.

In pre-colonial Aotearoa, Māori tribes, although sharing similar views and practices, regarded themselves as independent political bodies. Despite their genealogical, economic and military links, they guarded their independence jealously. My own people, Ngāti Hauā, co-existed with neighbouring Tainui tribes, Te Arawa and Hauraki peoples for hundreds of years. At times these tribes would work together on joint projects, and in times of conflict there were recognised processes to resolve problems. When the colonising settlers arrived in this country, they built homes they were familiar and comfortable with. These were built among the established Māori homes. The Māori neighbours believed that the homes could co-exist, in the way that neighbouring tribes had co-existed for centuries. Māori also saw mutual advantages in sharing and trading resources with a neighbour who brought benefits such as new crops, tools, animals and technologies into their communities.

The cornerstone of any society is its resource base. Without resources, a society cannot shelter its people, provide security and produce the necessities of life. As all the physical resources of Aotearoa were controlled and developed by Māori, early European traders, missionaries and settlers were heavily engaged in attaining resources to support their new homes.

The establishment of a Pākehā house changed the neighbourhood. The settlers who were to become Pākehā regarded themselves as superior and their society as better than that of their neighbours. Many believed it was appropriate for them to share what they saw as the superior benefits of Western civilisation with their Māori neighbours. If these benefits were unwanted and rejected by Māori, many of the Europeans asserted them anyway – as a 'civilising' force, often with arrogant insistence and, if challenged, with violence and force of arms.

By 1840 it was deemed necessary to negotiate an agreement between Māori leaders and new immigrants for peaceful settlement. It is estimated that at the time the Māori population was between 70,000 to 90,000 people, compared to a Pākehā population of around 2,000.[5] Within twenty years of the signing of this agreement, Te Tiriti o Waitangi or the Treaty of Waitangi, immigrant settlers outnumbered Māori, and as the settlers' need for land increased, conflict ensued. The establishment of a settler government, the land wars, resulting land confiscations, introduced diseases and a court system to deal with the transfer of Māori resources – as well as the halving of the Māori population by the early 1900s[6] – all contributed to the demise of Māori control. As Māori lost control over their resources, the Pākehā economy and communities were correspondingly strengthened. The newly established government justified its economic advantage by citing its 'democratic' majority – a majority that entrenched itself initially by excluding Māori from the franchise and then in 1867, once settlers outnumbered them, by marginalising Māori political power by effectively restricting them to four seats in Parliament. Once a numerical and institutional advantage was achieved, the military and police were able to enforce a set of laws to maintain Pākehā control.

The Treaty as a tool of colonisation might be compared to an abusive marriage. Your partner moves into your home, as agreed, but you soon find out he is not very nice. His ideas about your relationship revolve around domination, removing personal choices and aspirations you had. His denigrating behaviour causes you to lose confidence. You begin to believe the picture he builds up about who you are, and your status and sense of worth becomes reliant on your relationship with him. You remain committed to the relationship, but the benefits roll only one way, couched in paternalistic rhetoric: 'It is for your own good!' The abuser sees and openly describes himself to you and others as a gracious benefactor. He places constant pressure on you to justify his use and maintenance of power, and finds it difficult to hear an alternative view; he is genuinely surprised if challenged about the inequality of the relationship. In the same way, a dominant society *requires* a subaltern population to maintain its own ideas of itself.

Māori did not willingly give up their homes. They resisted politically, physically, culturally and spiritually. In 1861 Wiremu Tāmihana Tarapīpipi, the leading chief of Ngāti Hauā, accused the government of duplicity and argued for the equality of all nations and therefore the right of Māori people to maintain sovereignty. He asserted:

But is not the Queen a native of England, Nicholas, of Russia, Buonaparte, of France, and Pomare, of Tahiti, – each from his own people? Then why am I, or these tribes, rebuked by you, and told that we and you must unite together under the Queen. ... I of this island, am of a different race, not nearly connected. My only connection with you is through Christ (Ephes. 11.13.) Were all the different islands [countries] under one sovereignty, that of the Queen, it would be quite right, no one would differ; all this island would also be united with the rest. Instead of which, each nation is separate, and I also, standing here in my own thought, which is this – that I must have a King for myself.[7]

Tāmihana's global examples and the biblical reference demonstrates his awareness of the wider forces at play. He presents a universal argument based on information from the wider world. Tāmihana was also part of a pan-tribal network of Māori leaders debating and looking for solutions to problems created by colonisation. He believed that the establishment of a unified Māori body – a body of equal mana to Parliament – would give the necessary voice and strength to deal with a settler government. This led to his support for the Kīngitanga, the Māori King movement, through the mid to late 1850s and the anointing of the first kings, Pōtatau Te Wherowhero in 1858 and his son Tāwhiao in 1860. The response from the colonial government of the day to this show of Māori power was to invade Waikato in 1863, ultimately resulting in the confiscation of thousands of acres of land. Although this was done under the guise of punishing rebels, its true purpose was to make more land available to settlers.

In 1881 the Kīngitanga laid down its arms and sought to resolve differences through political negotiation with the state. This change of tack by the Kīngitanga recognised the military imbalance between the Crown and the Kīngitanga – in terms of the sheer numbers of potential fighters – and the desire of the Kīngitanga to open up peaceful political channels to resolve injustices. Despite this, the tribes faithful to the Kīngitanga progressively lost most of their land through confiscation.

Tāwhiao, the second Māori King, visited England in 1884 hoping to speak directly with his counterpart monarch Queen Victoria, but was disappointed to return without having found a just way forward. He summarised the trip in the saying 'I haere Māori atu, i hoki Māori mai' (I left as a Māori and returned a Māori), meaning that the visit did not change the circumstances of Māori.

There were many other Māori individuals and groups that challenged colonial power. These include Māori peaceful resistance movements, the most famous of which was established at the Taranaki settlement of Parihaka between the 1860s and 1880s under the leadership of Te Whiti o Rongomai and Tohu Kākahi. Others include the Kotahitanga movement that set up a Māori parliament in Waitangi in 1892 that attempted to unite Māori people; and the Young Māori Party, which believed working within European society would better support Māori. The Young Māori Party included noted lawyers, doctors, politicians and scholars, among them Āpirana Ngata, Māui Pōmare, James Carroll and Te Rangi Hīroa (Peter Buck), all four of whom were later knighted.[8] Tahupōtiki Wiremu Rātana's vision led in the early 1920s to a religious movement to revive the physical and spiritual condition of Māori people, and it grew strong political connections with the Labour Party, a relationship that has helped Labour gain parliamentary seats from the 1930s until today. Māori religious movements such as Pai Mārire (from the early 1860s) and Ringatū (from the mid-1860s) also drew from Māori beliefs and practices alongside Christianity, a signal that even the Māori soul wished to exist independently from the colonial system.

In order to justify their use of violence, the colonisers objectified Māori people and dismissed their practices as primitive, inferior, unintelligent, ignorant, uncivilised, violent, inhumane, and degrading to women. It was only after applying this subjugating discourse and their overwhelming force that Pākehā people were able to seize control. With this control they coerced Māori into building, living in and supporting the colonised form of their new home. The brutality of Pākehā dominance was evident in the way resistance groups of Māori people were killed, imprisoned, made destitute, separated from their families and lands, discredited, demonised and ridiculed.[9] This behaviour toward Māori was normalised and became the basis of a system built to benefit Pākehā by endowing them with wealth and privilege. Building a society on a foundation of violence – whether that is physical, legislative or social – creates an underclass of people. This is the hidden shame of New Zealand's founding which has affected the relationships between Māori and other New Zealanders ever since.

With no viable economy, limited political power, a foreign education system, poor health care and discriminatory law and justice, the consequent degradation of Māori language and customs was inevitable. Māori people could survive only by participating in New Zealand society as an unwelcome, disadvantaged minority. Māori leaders such as Āpirana Ngata and Te Rangi Hīroa believed Māori participation in the world wars would demonstrate Māori commitment to the nation, but despite suffering disproportionate losses, the movement of Māori from rural to urban areas in the 1950s and 1960s highlighted the discrimination latent in New Zealand society.[10] By the 1970s a previously flourishing, multi-dimensional Māori society existed only as hollowed-out remnants in rural pockets, often in impoverished communities; traditional cultural practices were observed in enclaves of Māori homes and marae on the margins of society. In the cities, Māori struggled to maintain connections with their tūrangawaewae, and their efforts to continue and forge new cultural practices were hampered by the economic constraints of life within the Pākehā system. The replacement of the Māori whare with the Pākehā house was complete. The Māori way of life and its belief system became regarded as a mere façade, retained only for its myths and legends, kapa haka entertainment and physical relics in museum displays.

Colonisation continues today in the ongoing protection of benefits by and for those who already have power and resources. For instance, current social indicators for Māori show a community under compounding pressure. Māori experience lower educational expectations and achievement, die on average ten years before Pākehā New Zealanders,[11] receive less effective medical care for treatable illnesses (and therefore have a lower survival rate) and are four to five times more likely than Pākehā to be sent to jail when appearing in the courts.[12] This pressure on fragile families and communities pushes them into cycles of poverty and self-harm that are difficult to break.

Living with the effects of colonisation – living in the coloniser's house – is like losing your voice, some would say. It's losing your own words, then struggling to understand your stories and how they used to make sense of the world we live in. Eventually colonised people are forced to use the words and the pictures that belong to the coloniser, giving a foreign interpretation of our reality. This extends to the very names we use to label our identities.

WHAT'S IN A NAME?

Along with making large-scale changes to Māori society, colonisation also touched the everyday practices and norms of Māori communities. Māori have adopted and adapted many customs that come from our colonial past – sometimes because they were forced to, sometimes because they chose to, sometimes simply because it was practical. In this process, Māori have come to accept many Pākehā customs.

Recently I was reading through our book of tribal genealogy which has literally hundreds of names of ancestors, over centuries. The book was begun in 1927, started by a great-grand-uncle, and has been passed down through the family. Names, in a society with an unwritten language prior to the arrival of Europeans, were used to retain important information for families. There are many examples of this in our history. The Ngāti Hauā chief Te Waharoa is said to have been born in the late 1700s and was named in remembrance of his father's death in the gateway of a hostile community. Te Waharoa and his relatives had an obligation to settle the imbalance caused by the death of their relative; in speaking the name 'Te Waharoa', the feelings relating to those events would be remembered.

Within the genealogy, I noticed that prior to European contact there were very few ancestral names repeated in hundreds of entries. However, in the post-contact lists of names, many introduced names – transliterated, often biblical – such as Wiremu (William), Hoani (John), Mere (Mary) and Hera (Sarah), began to recur. Christian missionaries in the 1800s encouraged their Māori converts to take baptismal names. Tarapīpipi – the king-making Ngāti Hauā chief I mentioned earlier – for example, became Wiremu Tāmihana, the Māori translation for William Thompson. These converts sometimes combined their Māori names with their Christian names, so Wiremu Tāmihana would use this name *and* Tarapīpipi. It doesn't look like my early Māori ancestors had a need for surnames, but later the European surname convention was adopted, drawing on the father's name as a surname. The full name of Tarapīpipi then became Wiremu Tāmihana Tarapīpipi Te Waharoa.

As time went by and Pākehā practices became more widely accepted, English names become more prevalent in the whakapapa. Māori transliterations were dropped and families began using English names. Although all of my mother's brothers and sisters were given Māori names at birth, most of them use English names. When I asked an aunt why this was, she told me that a Pākehā teacher at school in the 1950s found her name difficult to pronounce and called her Maureen instead, after a movie star at the time. The name stuck. How could a teacher possibly think they had the power to rename somebody else's child? Why would a family and community accept that behaviour? It is disconcerting. In recent years my aunt has begun introducing herself to people using her birth name. Interestingly, some family members choose not to use her Māori name, because of its pronunciation. This seemingly small act of reclaiming a Māori birth name, a remnant of a time when Māori named and mediated the world around us, has created an opportunity for uncomfortable but potentially transformative discussions about racism in our communities.

Interesting too is the adoption of the European custom of naming children after relatives. There is some evidence of this occurring among Māori prior to colonisation, but in reading the names of pre-colonisation ancestors, it seems not to have been the norm. The implications of these changes may not seem significant when we have so many other identity markers for individuals today – the language you speak, the kura you attend, the sport you play and support, the job you have, the place you live and the resources you have. However, it is another sign of colonial changes in the way Māori engage with the world.

Within my own family, members have found new and unique ways to name children, looking to black American culture or following the example of pop artists, while ignoring the rich tradition within our own culture. Battered by the forces of colonialism, perhaps our ancestors came to believe that whatever was good for Pākehā was good enough for Māori. So today the Māori King movement refers to Tūheitia the current King as 'Pōtatau Te Wherowhero VII', a grand title that encompasses the names of the previous six kings and queen. In some ways Māori make firmer efforts in maintaining Pākehā tradition today than our colonial cousins do.

BEING PĀKEHĀ, BEING MĀORI?

It was widely assumed within the Pākehā house that Māori would quickly see the advantages of living in the Pākehā manner. A sense of cultural superiority led Pākehā to think the European style of living was, on balance, a better way to live. The fact that 'civilised' Western Europe had prospered from colonisation and controlled most of the occupied world was taken to be a sign of that superiority. Although Māori were quick to adopt ideas and practices from Europeans – as with the naming practices discussed above – Māori used these things to advance *Māori* society. Mistakenly, many Pākehā interpreted that as Māori wanting to be Pākehā, and the misinterpretation persists in many quarters.

Instead, Māori – and some Pākehā – are disillusioned and confused by the promises made about the benefits of living in a society where Pākehā justice, education, health, culture and language have proven to be detrimental for Māori well-being. A Māori solution is to rebuild and live in a place of their own. We know this because the agitation by Māori to preserve, maintain and re-establish themselves is both historic and ongoing. To quote my ancestor Wiremu Tāmihana: 'Kāore aku kī kia whiu atu a Kuini i tēnei motu, engari ko taku pīhi ko au te kaitfrom i taku pīhi' (It is not my intention to throw out the Queen from this land, only that in my piece I have authority over my piece).[13] This was a statement of independence through interdependence, recognising the separate authority of each party.

More recent examples of this include concerns around the loss of Māori language expressed since the 1970s, the Waitangi Tribunal settlements from the 1990s and initiatives in broadcasting, education, health and justice that have all led to greater government support for Māori philosophy and practices in those fields. Māori interests, values and language are becoming more visible and accessible to many New Zealanders.

These initiatives are aimed at addressing the crises for Māori in justice, health, housing, employment and the economy, and are often promoted amongst decision-makers as the basis of a fair and just society – equality of opportunity and support for all citizens regardless of their race or creed. Among those who count the financial cost of inequality, addressing social ills also makes good financial sense. For example, using the hundred thousand dollars[14] it costs to jail someone for a year could be better used in preventative or support programmes and would produce better outcomes than a prison sentence. However, although many of these programmes are important and logical drivers for addressing social problems, they often assume a socialisation of Māori into Pākehā systems and they ignore the choice increasingly being made by Māori to create or adapt systems whereby Māori themselves determine both the problems and vehicles to solve them. In the chapters to follow, we will see other examples of how decision-making by Māori for Māori can help unravel the effects of long-established colonial structures and institutions.

Although being caught in the throat of the Parata is a terrifying experience for travellers, at times even with the best planning this force of nature cannot be avoided. It is the resilience and capacity of those people within the canoe that determine what state it will be in after the storm. The process of colonisation has consistently and continuously attacked and destroyed many of the foundations of Māori society, seeking to replace one house with another. Māori resistance has also been consistent and continuous, although battling from an impoverished and fragmented position. Māori want to live as Māori within the world as it is today.[15]

2. WHAT IS DECOLONISATION?

OCEAN RIPEKA MERCIER
(NGĀTI POROU)

As discussed by Mike in Chapter 1, colonisation transforms a land and a society in profound ways. Its imposition of alien political and social structures leaves deep impressions and scars on landscapes and on peoples. The ongoing process of colonisation, and the mental and emotional weight of coloniality, take a toll on colonised people like Māori – what and how they know and think, their health, lifeways and spirit. While others, like most Pākehā, may enjoy the comfort of the colonial framework, even the least impacted of us may have a sense of unease, a sense that something is not quite right (as will be discussed more fully by Rebecca in the next chapter). Where inequity exists in a society, all suffer, not just the oppressed.

But those who have experienced or realised the enormous systems-wide, environmental, social, mental, emotional and spiritual impact of colonisation may come to ask: how can we change things? Is *de*colonisation the natural solution? If so, how might we begin to make changes in such a complex network? What even is this six-syllable mouthful of a word?

We'll start this chapter with some simple definitions. This will lead us to a short discussion on the 'colony ups and leaves' kind of decolonisation that the dictionaries know about – the prospect of which people find unsettling in the New Zealand context. Scholars have been writing about decolonisation for decades, so we'll survey some international and local ideas. Many of these writers are Indigenous, reflecting the hope that is felt amongst native researcher communities for decolonisation as an emancipatory or freeing pathway. In these works, decolonisation is mostly discussed in the same breath as liberation, transformation, power, Indigenous agency and 'efforts to create space for Indigenous people and knowledge'.[1] In a country such as Aotearoa, in which Te Tiriti o Waitangi has mediated settler–native relations, we might say that decolonisation is underpinned by a commitment to making cohabitation work.

These are lofty goals, but not everyone has the same ideas about how we achieve them. Nor are the methods in one area fit for another. Like a big DIY house renovation in which we restore the house that was colonised (see Chapter 1), not all jobs can be done at once or with the same tools. Gutters are usually tackled separately from removing pests from the roof space, and it's a bad idea to refurbish your kitchen and your bathroom at the same time. Furthermore, some of the tasks are sequential: in order to paint the walls, some of the weatherboards might need replacing first – and you'd better not skip the primer. Similarly, different disciplinary areas – land, ecological systems, the mind, research methods, education, physical spaces and so on – have developed different understandings and mechanisms for doing decolonisation.

Very basically, decolonisation involves rethinking and then action. Educational theorist Graham Hingangaroa Smith puts it as conscientisation, resistance and transformative action.[2] The thinking begins with a recognition of colonisation in all its forms and guises. If you don't know what your own house looked like, how can you recognise what's different about the colonial house? Decolonisation involves critical self-reflection and outward observation; it seeks to embody pre-colonial, Indigenous and non-colonial paradigms; it unearths and addresses embedded colonial thinking. Decolonisation, then, takes individual and collaborative action to root out the weeds of colonisation and provide space for Indigenous ways of knowing and being – and more besides. All together, these actions can lead to radical personal and societal change.

Finally, this chapter will consider the pitfalls for aspiring decolonisers and the pushback we might encounter. This includes overt opposition, the colonisation of Indigenisation, succumbing to our internal colonisers, variations on old colonisation and the evolution of colonisation into something new. How do we know our decolonial efforts are not contributing to further colonisation? The colonial project is so pervasive and subtle that it can sometimes co-opt our decolonisation without our realising it. Finally, the chapter asks if 'decolonisation' really *is* the best way to describe this emancipatory project; and what our houses and neighbourhoods might look like once a decolonial liberation has been achieved.

While I have written the chapter on the premise that decolonisation definitely isn't a project just for Indigenous peoples, I leave it for Amanda in Chapter 4 to explore the specific role of non-Indigenous allies.[3]

A DECOLONISATION DRESS REHEARSAL
Pat and I got engaged and then married while this book was being conceived and written. We wanted to bring our own personalities and heritages to the wedding, and to express our connections to this

whenua from having lived in Aotearoa for more than a century between us. As te taiao-oriented, environmentally conscious people – Pat's mission in life is to expunge old man's beard and rats from the forests of Aotearoa – we wanted our wedding to include gentle and suggestive acts of ecological decolonisation. How might design elements that celebrate Aotearoa's Indigenous traditions take over a wedding? And how could we express these sensibilities when we were getting married in a manicured country garden more reminiscent of England or Japan than Aotearoa?

Aotearoa's native species have suffered wave upon wave of colonisation by pest species – plant, animal and sometimes human. We are all environmentally and culturally poorer for the decimation and extinction of our natives. Exotic gardens can be poignant reminders of these losses – where hīnau berries used to be harvested, flowering cherry trees now thrive. Our wedding venue needed serious decolonisation, and – given that a full restoration of the Indigenous landscape wasn't feasible – we decided on a symbolic takeover by native species and Māori design elements as a dress rehearsal to this decolonisation. We hid sculptures of kōkako, tūī, kererū and ruru in the gardens for our guests to find. Our invitations, flowers and cake used harakeke and whāriki flax. Te reo Māori was read and heard during our ceremony and reception.

A groomsman adorned our bridal bower with toetoe, and a breeze sent its seed wafting through the air in search of a new home.

But what happened to our (re)decorations after the wedding? We didn't own the gardens, we merely rented them for ten hours. Those who marry on whānau land have room to put up a marquee and decorate at will. Their long-term connection to the land may run as deeply as their own whakapapa. In a sense, they have been 'decorating' for years and years – whether that is building, landscaping, planting or creating memories from other occasions. They can leave their embellishments up for as long as they like and be surrounded by those remembrances for as long as they choose. We had a photographic record of our day at the hired venue, but had made no lasting impact on it. Our decorative endeavour might have been useful practice, but was a bit sad as a permanent attempt at decolonisation.

Nonetheless, it affirmed our identities in various ways. These included nods to our Dutch and English heritage – tulips made from harakeke in the bridal bouquet, constructed roses. I am Māori, but I have settler/coloniser ancestry as well. So, while decolonising was my focus, in planning I found myself thinking in whakapapa mode. This way of working acknowledges intertwined identities and histories. It meant I could draw from them all, but also gave me a licence to privilege parts of the story over others – and would give me a personal stake and responsibility in any endeavour.

There are a few issues I seek to raise with this flowery story. One is about our currently limited sovereignty over whenua. Another is about the efforts we make to paper over the surface impacts of colonisation. These might raise consciousness, but won't necessarily produce lasting physical change. Another point is that sometimes a decolonising paradigm can be exhausting and personally disempowering. A whakapapa paradigm, by contrast – which has deep connections to relationships with and stories in the land – gives one the power to make decisions about which traditions and histories should be privileged at any given moment.

DEFINITIONS AND UNDERSTANDINGS, IN AOTEAROA AND ELSEWHERE

Like colonisation, decolonisation is a huge and amorphous project.[4] Some commentators and workers on decolonisation will jump into a room and start the clean-up without stopping to think about the bigger picture: what's going on next door and in the project as a whole. The upshot of this is that a reader of decolonisation literature is generally assumed to know what is meant by 'decolonisation'. Many writers only loosely define what they mean by it, and others use it as a general black box for addressing the negative impacts of colonisation upon Indigenous peoples.

Problems abound. As Brendan Hokowhitu of the University of Waikato puts it, decolonisation is a

worthy project, yet we must at least question the semantics of the project of 'decolonisation'; what does that actually mean and, if we could ever define it, is it actually possible?[5]

A worthy project, a tricky thing to define and perhaps even unrealisable: how the word 'decolonisation' is understood in different parts of the world will depend on the specific local relationship between colony and colonised. The online *Oxford English Dictionary* defines it as 'the withdrawal from its former colonies of a colonial power; the acquisition of political or economic independence by such colonies'.[6] This withdrawal may have been voluntary, or forced by social, political and environmental pressures. Other definitions of 'decolonise' include 'to grant independence to a colony',[7] 'to allow [a colony] to become self-governing or independent'[8] and 'to free from colonial status'.[9] The *Merrium-Webster Dictionary* notes that the word's first known use was in 1963. While the term may have an uncertain but relatively recent provenance, decolonisation itself is not a new thing, as many authors state.[10]

The kinds of decolonisation which involve a technical independence and freedom have been discussed by authors such as Frantz Fanon and Ngũgĩ wa Thiong'o.[11] These states of autonomy and independence tend to occur after a literal removal of the colonial power from the colonised nation state. Many northern nations – particularly Great Britain, France, Portugal and Belgium, as well as the United States – from the sixteenth to nineteenth centuries colonised different parts of Africa, Asia and the global south, some of which went on to be decolonised, largely in the twentieth century. The central African country Cameroon, for instance – variously occupied as German Kamerun, French Cameroun and British Cameroons – gained independence from its British and European colonisers in 1960–61, after four decades of struggle and resistance. Or take Indonesia: colonised by the Dutch as the Dutch East Indies in the 1800s and recognised as independent in 1949. Closer to home, decolonisation of Pacific nations has also occurred in the past century: Samoa gained independence in 1962, Fiji in 1970, Vanuatu in 1980.[12]

This process sometimes leaves states in a colonised mindset, with ongoing differences and division. In the case of Indonesia, the decolonised became colonisers in turn, taking over the colonial role in nations such as Timor Leste and West Papua. As writer and critic Lana Lopesi has suggested, a colonised mind leads to colonisation of others.[13] Similarly, artificial lines drawn on maps by British and European colonisers may bear little resemblance to traditional boundaries and homelands, leaving newly independent states made up of many different peoples – some allies, some rivals, some forcibly relocated from elsewhere to provide labour for colonisers. Citizens of states with these differing groups of people, such as Nigeria or Fiji, may thus remain locked in contestation over power.[14] And though independent in name, newly decolonised states can struggle for economic independence, relying on old colonial relationships for aid, development and trading partners. This form of decolonisation, then, is far from a true reversal of colonisation or rehabilitation from colonial ills, though it may be a heartening and necessary first step.

For our purposes, there are other problems with it as a model. 'Independence' decolonisation has been most often applied to countries where the coloniser population was small or temporary, where the Indigenous peoples remained in the majority. In settler countries like Canada, Australia and Aotearoa New Zealand, the reality is different and more complex. The above definitions of decolonisation speak of a literal removal of the colonising people and the powers that uphold colonial structures. Little wonder, then, that many

New Zealanders see decolonisation as a bit scary. Take this entry on a recent blogpost:

Talking about the effects of colonisation is important, but I don't think that throwing potentially divisive terms like decolonisation into the discussion help. We all have to work together on this, an us and them attitude is unlikely to fix anything.[15]

This person, like many, worries that decolonisation is potentially divisive, fearing an 'us' versus 'them' mentality. However, we might argue that, just as Māori identity grew here in Aotearoa, Pākehā identity also belongs nowhere else (as is explored more fully in the next chapters). While not ready to confer something like tangata whenua status on Pākehā, most Māori do acknowledge that Pākehā identity is now a part of New Zealand culture. In the meantime, while some Pākehā fear that decolonisation will require removal of the coloniser (whoever that coloniser is), the decolonisation we want to talk about will rarely if ever call for that.

This type of decolonisation does, however, suggest that the systems we work within need major overhaul. As Indigenous studies scholars Waziyatawin Angela Wilson and Michael Yellow Bird state:

We are not advocating the immediate taking up of arms or the organization of an Indigenous militia. Instead, we are advocating peaceful, intelligent and courageous challenges to the existing institutions of colonialism as well as questioning our own complicity in those institutions. But make no mistake: Decolonization ultimately requires the overturning of the colonial structure. It is not about tweaking the existing colonial system to make it more Indigenous-friendly or a little less oppressive. The existing system is fundamentally and irreparably flawed. We hope the decolonization strategies we offer will help Indigenous communities become increasingly more sophisticated and fundamentally challenging to the current power structure as we strengthen and prepare ourselves for our long struggle toward complete liberation.[16]

The online Urban Dictionary suggests that to decolonise is '[a] verb justifying an African school of thought regarding the removal of any Western ideas in a social, political or scientific issue. Logic is optional.'[17] This definition (when stripped of its offensive edge) is in line with our idea of decolonisation, in that it doesn't focus on a literal movement or 'shooing out' of the coloniser. In the Aotearoa context and in many other settler states – such as Hawai'i, the mainland United States, Canada and Australia – decolonising does not mean the removal or withdrawal of colonial occupiers so much as a fundamental shift in the ideas, knowledges and value sets that underpin the systems which shape our country.

In Aotearoa, Te Tiriti o Waitangi of 1840 cements an ongoing relationship of mutual benefit between hapū and the British Crown. Signed by 400-plus rangatira and Crown representatives, it is an agreement that hapū Māori have honoured. By contrast (as we saw in Chapter 1), the Crown's breaches have been numerous and ongoing, resulting in confiscation or lack of protection of land and resources, and displacement of people. The Treaty settlements process – which involves an apology, compensation and return of land in Crown ownership – does not and has never uprooted New Zealand residents from privately owned land, contrary to the impressions of some Pākehā.[18] In the Aotearoa context, writings about land decolonisation tend to focus on reversing the damaging effects of large-scale industrial, horticultural and pastoral activities. Long-term native species preservation, reforestation, and weed and pest control efforts – encapsulated by the Predator-Free 2050 goal – can also be framed as ecological decolonisation.

The point should be made, however, that while decolonisation discourse in Aotearoa is almost never about the removal of people, decolonisation is not just a metaphor.[19] It should not be treated merely as a consciousness-raising device. A decade ago, Indigenous studies researchers Eve Tuck and K. Wayne Yang observed decolonising discourse being appropriated: used by non-Indigenous individuals to demarcate their identity from other colonisers and to signal alliance. While some strides in the process of decolonisation might be achieved through small 'right-shifting' actions[20] – and such shifts should be encouraged and applauded – actions such as driving around with a 'Decolonise the World' bumper sticker or sporting a 'Decoloniser' t-shirt may undermine its meaning and impact, especially when big companies are quick to appropriate symbols of revolution to sell their gear and brand.[21]

Rather than being a slogan, virtue signal or metaphor, the decolonisation we discuss in this book seeks to maintain a focus on 'repatriation of Indigenous land and life'.[22] It doesn't necessitate the wholesale withdrawal of 'the coloniser', but does require that power imbalances are addressed, that negative effects of colonisation are peeled away and that pre-colonial ways are revived – often starting with language, education and social practices or tikanga. As Māori academic Ngahuia Murphy explains, decolonisation is

about confronting a continuing colonial agenda that manifests itself in myriad ways. These include the denial of our right to autonomy as indigenous peoples, the self-hatred that thrives in our communities as a consequence of ethnocidal policies that attempted to stamp out our philosophies and practices, and the relentless plundering of our elders – the land, the sea, the forests and rivers – under the banner of 'progress', 'civilisation' and 'development'.[23]

As mentioned in Chapter 1, we think Moana Jackson's house metaphor is useful and evocative, and through the rest of this chapter we'll use whare and houses to illustrate different points. First up, though, we need to get things in the right order. You might go to the trouble of painting the house and hanging the wallpaper, and then realise a complete overhaul and redesign is needed. In the next section, we'll instead take time to dream, scheme, imagine and plan.

WHERE DOES DECOLONISATION HAPPEN? IN THE MIND

While decolonisation is a process – a multi-dimensional web of active steps – much attention has been paid to the cognitive processes that *precede* such actions. Here I'll start by discussing this mind-work.

Like anything that is new and paradigm-shifting – not remote, robotic or automatic – decolonisation first begins in the mind. This thinking will take stock and reflect on the way things are. Many workers in decolonisation are motivated to change-based thought by the realisation that the status quo is oppressive – and this realisation may come as a shock to the system. The 'cultural bomb' of colonisation, for instance – as Ngũgĩ wa Thiong'o terms it in the influential book *Decolonising the Mind*[24] – can turn a culture from a vibrant living thing into shrapnel. Ngũgĩ notes that the point of impact of this bomb must become the foundation for picking up the pieces and pushing for change.

Similarly, Paulo Freire in his 1968 book *Pedagogy of the Oppressed* emphasises *praxis*: 'reflection and action upon the world in order to transform it'.[25] This state of reflection allows one to go from subjugated human being to liberated human being:

[D]ecolonizing actions must begin in the mind, and that creative, consistent, decolonized thinking shapes and empowers the brain, which in turn provides a major prime for position change. Undoing the effects of colonialism and working toward decolonization requires each of us to consciously consider to what degree we have been affected by not only the physical aspects of colonization, but also the psychological, mental and spiritual aspects.[26]

Michael Yellow Bird's conceptual model of decolonisation in *For Indigenous Eyes Only: A Decolonization Handbook* describes it as an event *and* a process. The event is notable – it is the moment one reaches a critical level of consciousness.[27] Being at this level of consciousness involves a kind of hair-raising realisation. It leads to action. Involved in this action, or process, are activities of creating, restoring and devising, and enacting strategies to liberate.

Hawaiian sovereignty leader Pōkā Laenui, in his important essay 'Processes of Decolonization', envisages a decolonisation process of five stages that also reveals the importance of decolonising the mind.[28] In fact, his first four steps – Rediscovery and recovery, Mourning, Dreaming, and Commitment – are cognitive processes.[29] Of his fifth stage, Action, he makes the point that sometimes a community whose survival is at imminent risk may be forced to act. In this case, the community must forgo the luxury of rediscovery, dreaming and commitment. (Laenui's five stages were inspired in turn by the five stages of colonisation that were theorised by Filipino psychologist Virgilio Enriquez: Denial and withdrawal, Destruction/Eradication, Denigration/Belittlement/Insult, Surface accommodation/Tokenism, and Transformation/Exploitation – of which more later.)[30]

Another early step in decolonisation is to shine a light on the effects of colonisation, recognising, naming and quantifying its impact. In New Zealand, discrepancies are well documented in statistics on Māori life expectancy, imprisonment, education, employment and income levels, housing situation – the list goes on. At a personal level, decolonisation 'involves a reflective peeling back of various layers of privilege and the ignorance that comes with it'.[31] Other authors talk about peeling away coloniality like a close-fitting skin.

My own educational experience was a bit different from that of many Māori, including

Bianca's. I loved school and always did well. I didn't perceive any low (or high) expectations on me. I've had good role models and encouraging teachers. However, it wasn't until I started working in Māori studies in my late twenties that I began to appreciate how deeply Western or Pākehā my mind had become. It explained why I had feelings of relief, rather than indignation, when I heard people say I was 'different from those other Māori'. I'd become that 'good Māori', one who can operate as a Pākehā, comfortable in colonising systems – education in particular, and physics, no less!

Shortly after I'd gained my bachelor's degree in physics and maths, someone at the ceremony asked, 'Where does she get her intelligence from?' Mum interjected with a smile: 'She gets it from my side.' I interpreted Dad's silent response to mean 'Of course not, but I'll humour her.' Now, my dad's parents are from Cornwall: Grampa had a divinity degree and was a vicar in different Anglican parishes in England and the Rangitīkei, and Gran had a degree in home economics and was a teacher. Mum's parents are from Tikitiki. When they moved to Wellington, Nana and Grumps worked as labourers in the Ford factory and, when it closed down, the Griffin's biscuit factory. So while I'd never dare disagree with Mum openly, I could relate to Dad's scepticism. My Pākehā side was the smart side, and that's where I got my intelligence.

I had believed this my whole life. My schooling had been complicit in teaching me to equate work experience, degrees and perceptions of what is 'civilised' with intelligence.

I'd completely overlooked the mātauranga held by my kaumātua. Grumps was so humble about it that I learned only later that he taught at Te Aute College. Nana caught eels with skill and reference to the maramataka,[32] and practised rongoā Māori. This was indeed kind of a hair-raising realisation, a peeling back of ignorance and a recognition of privilege. It's only quite recently that I've realised the enduring impact of racist and wrongheaded concepts such as phrenology[33] and miscegenation on my upbringing. My corresponding resolve, or action, is mahi to raise the value of mātauranga into general consciousness.

HOW DOES DECOLONISATION HAPPEN? IT'S A PROCESS

Pōkā Laenui's first stage of decolonisation, Rediscovery and recovery,[34] describes revitalisation of old ways, te mahi a ngā tūpuna. As Ngahuia Murphy puts it, 'Decolonisation to me is about healing, clearing, releasing, transforming, remembering, reviving and reasserting the pathways of our tīpuna (ancestors).'[35] Strengthening pre- and extra-colonial ways is important because it provokes a shift in the dominant voice, message and medium. Revitalisation calls for redirection of focus and effort, allowing suppressed knowledges to be untangled and freed. These can be expressed and reclaimed in many ways.

Education has been one important site for revitalisation. Imported education systems were a key mechanism in the colonisation of Indigenous minds, implicated in the assimilation of native children and their families.[36] A revitalised, decolonised education system might seek to recover plurality, or different ways of knowing. It would 'take back power' at multiple levels. Moana Jackson has asked: 'how do we educate for rangatiratanga?' and 'what options are available to us to ensure the sort of colonisation-free rangatiratanga-embracing education that our tamariki are entitled to?'[37] The revitalisation of education systems also goes hand in hand with Kaupapa Māori.[38] Kaupapa Māori is both a response to colonialism and an expression of Māoritanga in education. It is a decades-old movement linked to the setting up of kōhanga reo by parents who wanted their tamariki to be educated in te reo Māori. Māori scholars in academia, particularly education, were instrumental in this awakening. Decolonisation efforts like this continue to grow in early childhood, primary, secondary, tertiary and adult education.

As the kōhanga reo parents knew, language is a key route for ideas to be implanted in the mind, and decolonising work in Aotearoa is often seen in the elevation, revitalisation, use and normalising of te reo Māori. One of the most visible examples of this is in the restoration and renewal of Māori names. These might be corrections to corrupted versions of place names, as in the case of Whanganui (Wanganui) and Remutaka (Rimutaka), in which incorrect transcriptions and spellings had been made by settlers whose ears were unaccustomed to te reo Māori.

They could be old names brought back – around my own city of Te Whanganui-a-Tara, for instance, there are Matiu/Somes Island and Ahumairangi (Tinakori Hill). Or they could be new or reclaimed names: Pukehinau, a traditional name for the region occupied by the suburb of Kelburn in Wellington, is now being used for Lambton Ward. They could be the name of a person,[39] building, organisation, Crown or other entity, or business. Te Papa, for instance, has been completely naturalised and few now use the 'Museum of New Zealand' part of its name. Civic Square in central Wellington has been gifted the name Te Ngākau by Te Ātiawa mana whenua. And as part of name change and rebranding work, Victoria University of Wellington is now often citing its new Māori name, Te Herenga Waka, first. As educator Takawai Murphy has said, 'Reclaiming a Māori name became a simple but powerful gesture, a symbol of commitment to the path of healing, decolonisation and cultural reclamation.'[40]

Pōkā Laenui's second stage of decolonisation is Mourning. In this phase, injustice, trauma and losses are acknowledged and confronted. Healing can take place in this stage, but just as grief goes through many states, healing should also be produced from ongoing action in further stages. Mourning is an important stage, but Laenui cautions against becoming stuck in it, perpetuating one's feelings of victimisation.

The third stage in Laenui's decolonisation process is Dreaming, which invites us to imagine a decolonised reality in which contemporary truths and stories are acknowledged and drawn upon, to strengthen what has been revitalised or reawakened. He describes this step as most crucial for a 'true decolonisation', by which he means that Indigenous peoples should not simply occupy coloniser positions and replicate colonising structures.

True decolonization is more than simply replacing indigenous or previously colonized people into the positions held by colonizers. Decolonization includes the reevaluation of the political, social, economic and judicial structures themselves, and the development, if appropriate, of new structures which can hold and house the values and aspirations of the colonized people.[41]

Albert Wendt imagines a new Oceania 'free of the taint of colonialism'.[42] Such imagining is a form of Dreaming.

Commitment and Action are the final two stages in Laenui's schema. As I discuss below, the colonial machine and its blanketing mentalities is an exhausting, all-encompassing thing to break free of, and decolonisation cannot be achieved without persistence and commitment (in the New Zealand context this is often referred to as 'struggle without end').[43] Then, once an aspiring decoloniser is committed, action is imperative. Decolonising actions range from simple, personal day-to-day changes, to society-wide collective endeavours; they can be a matter of small subtle choices or loud public protest; they can be back-end research or frontline outcomes; they can be direct actions by citizens or mediated by political parties or other organisations.

As mentioned above, the development of Kaupapa Māori has been one of the most important decolonising actions in Aotearoa to date. First established in the field of education, it has since become widely used in other disciplines as a critical exploration and expression of Māori identity. Kaupapa Māori is work that is performed by Māori, about Māori and for Māori. It seeks transformative outcomes for whānau, hapū and iwi. Whanaungatanga (relationality) is critically important, and as such the field embraces subjectivity and eschews objectivity. Kaupapa Māori methodology emerged from critical and feminist theory (amongst others), and so it is also occupied with speaking truth to oppression from hegemony (dominance and complete control by a nation over others) and single, monolithic truths. While to some extent users of Kaupapa Māori theory and methods can pick and choose the aspects that suit their context, Kaupapa Māori without doubt has a decolonising agenda.[44]

One of the key figures in the Kaupapa Māori movement is Linda Tuhiwai Smith. Her book *Decolonizing Methodologies: Research and Indigenous Peoples*,[45] now into its third edition, has become a seminal text, locally and globally. The place- and people-specific application of Kaupapa Māori and its decolonising and indigenising principles mean that it strongly resonates with Indigenous peoples everywhere.[46] Smith herself has said her work and research is about using knowledge for the future:

When Cook arrived what began was a systematic destruction. Not only of what we knew, but the value of knowledge to us. And I hope in my work I've rebuilt confidence of Māori in our own knowledge. In our ability to know. To know well. To know deeply. And to know in ways that advance our future.[47]

We might argue that the decolonising action of Kaupapa Māori gains its freest and fullest expression in places that are largely independent of colonial systems. These may be our marae. They could be our educational spaces: the kōhanga reo, kura kaupapa or whare wānanga. Or they could be our homes, as educator and TV presenter Scotty Morrison has argued.[48] That these places are often reo-only zones is a significant emblem of this movement, although research in modern Māori suggests that even te reo Māori learners and speakers have to actively work against using English grammatical structures within their kōrero.

To see a truly decolonised Aotearoa, however, decolonising actions will also have to transform the European systems and frameworks that are the deep institutions of colonisation. One example is in the justice system, increasingly recognised as coloniality at work: colonisation keeps Māori disproportionately behind bars. The advocacy of Moana Jackson, youth-led movement JustSpeak and others in advocating for the abolition of prisons is a bold act of decolonisation. Clearly the disproportionate numbers of Māori in prisons isn't just because Māori are more likely to be 'bad' people; other things are going on here. Imprisoning more and more Māori is not a sustainable way forward. As Smith says, self-determination, decolonisation and social justice go together.[49] A decolonised society, therefore, should aim to be a just society.

In order to reach this just society, we will also need to decolonise the built environment of Aotearoa (as we explored in Imagining Decolonised Cities, the project that sparked this book).[50] For many Māori, urban environments symbolise pain: the pain of having lost whenua and having the city grow up around and take over traditional habitations. For others whose tūrangawaewae is elsewhere, cities can be places of disconnection from tribal roots (as discussed by Mike in Chapter 1); places where language and culture were lost due to government policies such as pepperpotting, where Māori whānau were distributed around cities to encourage them to assimilate to a Pākehā way of life. An urban decolonisation process might help alleviate this pain, enabling Māori whānau to live collectively in papakāinga-type arrangements. A number of urban papakāinga are now being developed in ways that speak to Māori values such as kaitiakitanga, as well as allowing hapū to live collectively and share resources.[51] However, legal tools that privilege private land ownership and funding mechanisms that make it very hard to borrow money on collectively owned land make this type of house building very hard to do.[52] In this area, decolonisation would involve a revamp of government supports to enable Māori to live on their whenua in good-quality homes.

Designers can help too. Public spaces are

important sites for decolonising acts. These may be small – such as providing diving platforms like the one on the Wellington waterfront that enable any teenager, whether or not they can afford to go to a pool, to have fun and show off their bombing prowess to passers-by. (If you ever find yourself down at the waterfront on a summer's day you may notice that many of the rangatahi jumping are Māori and Pasifika.) Other small acts might be making sure everyday signs are bilingual or in some way reference Māoriness – thus making Māoriness māori, or normal, in the civic space.[53]

The system of government used in New Zealand is another key institution of colonisation. In this book's final chapter, Moana discusses how decolonisation efforts might lead to a different constitutional arrangement for Aotearoa in a decolonised future. And as well as the changes under way in the fields of justice, education and the built environment, decolonisation work will need to be enacted in the multitude of other areas in Aotearoa that are built on deeply colonial foundations – our business, political and media structures, health and mental health organisations, systems of land tenure and conservation, and so on. Sometimes this may involve the complete transformation of systems and organisations along Indigenous lines, a rebuilding from the ground up; other times it may see useful Western concepts and systems repurposed and used in a Māori way, for Indigenous ends – like using the odd European building material in our restored whare.

HOW DOES DECOLONISATION 'UNHAPPEN'?

We live in a settler-colonial society which incessantly reminds us of its presence. The work of decolonising thought, knowledge, methods, pedagogies and all the rest, goes against the grain. It is an uphill hike. It needs constant attention, vigilance and effort. As with weaving, if decolonisation work stops, the work unravels. This unhappening – or *de*decolonising, if you will – occurs in numerous ways. This section discusses some of the many ways that coloniality can win out over decolonising work. We must be on guard for continuing coloniality (including claims that we are 'past all that' – i.e., a denial of colonisation's existence) and active pushback on attempts to decolonise.

The internal coloniser

If our minds are contaminated with self-hatred and the belief that we are inferior to our colonizers, we will believe in both the necessity and virtue of our own colonization.[54]

Colonisation and the 'civilisation' of natives are at their most effective when the natives are (by force, by law or by persuasion) convinced that colonisers bring a better, preferable way of living, and thus are willing to adopt coloniser ways and be assimilated. This acquiescence requires either an internal conviction or a capitulation. If I am convinced of the superiority of the coloniser – perhaps it is their arts, technology and science that win me over; their physical exoticism; or even their food (in my early years I was convinced that Gran's English cuisine was inherently more sophisticated than hāngī, boil-up, fried bread, steamed pudding and misshapen Mallowpuffs) – then invariably I will compare the artefacts of my Māori heritage to those of the coloniser, and find the Māori examples wanting. Furthermore, as these comparisons are usually adjudicated by coloniser standards, the colonising side is always more likely to come out on top. As a result, an Indigenous person in this situation may grow to despise their language, culture and heritage. The line from Malcolm X's famous speech 'Who taught you to hate the colour of your skin?' reminds us that these observations are not real but a *teaching*.[55] The speech affirms that what was taught can be unlearned.

Personal resistance to conforming and capitulating to the norms of the coloniser are thus key acts of decolonisation. In deciding whether and how to resist, we may need the luxury of time and reflection. Or we may have to make these evaluations on a moment-by-moment basis. Mum and I have not always pronounced 'Karori' (the suburb where we live) with rolled Rs and clipped syllables – and when we do now, we often get blank looks and have to resort to mispronunciation in order to be understood. Correct pronunciation of Māori words, using Māori greetings and Māori words in common discourse, and speaking Māori with Māori speakers are often not default positions and take effort to maintain. When we lapse into former habits of not doing these things, we're reminded that internal colonisation is still at work.

Another scenario where our internalized colonizers tend to surface is when we take positive steps to decolonize. No matter what type of steps we take, the more decolonizing they are, the more they are resisted at micro and macro levels – and not only from our dominant-society colonizers. Our decolonization methodologies must therefore be prepared to handle resistance from both the dominant society and, at times, our own community members.[56]

While we have power over our own internal coloniser, we can't directly control others' responses (nor should we try!). Whether resistance comes from our own minds or from slow-to-change mainstream attitudes, the key – according to those engaged in Treaty, te reo and tikanga workshops or even decolonisation training – is to 'decolonise hearts'.[57]

The colonisation of Indigenisation

As we saw above, making an effort to restore Indigenous ways and knowledges is a key strand of decolonisation.[58] Some argue that 'Indigenisation' is a better way to describe decolonial Indigenous activity, as the word etymologically avoids putting the coloniser at the centre; and others use the two in the same breath – that Indigenising is part of the decolonising project.[59] In the New Zealand context, Moana Jackson has called this 'reMāorification'.[60]

However, these ideas can bring other tensions. Is Indigenising simply new wallpaper on old walls? For example, Indigenising our justice system might simply produce (to use a North American example) 'a shackle lined with cotton' – it's 'still a shackle'.[61] Worse, Indigenisation may even be co-opted to reinforce colonialism. In Tokenism, Virgilio Enriquez's fourth step of colonisation (as described by Laenui), the coloniser displays tolerance and benevolence by giving 'surface accommodation' to the 'remnants of culture' belonging to the colonised people: 'They are tolerated as an exhibition of the colonial regime's sense of leniency to the continuing ignorance of the Natives.'[62] A recent change in the name of the government agency Child, Youth and Family, for example, to Oranga Tamariki, was met with derision. Given the way that Māori are treated within that very system (as mentioned by

Mike in Chapter 1),[63] Māori were right to call out the renaming as tokenism.

In the fifth step of colonisation, Transformation/Exploitation occurs: 'The traditional culture which simply refuses to die or go away is transformed into the culture of the dominating society.'[64] We can find local examples of this phenomenon. The Royal Society of New Zealand Te Apārangi, for instance, is one of various bodies using the practical policy called Vision Mātauranga to 'unlock the innovation potential of Māori knowledge, resources and people'. This sounds like an act of Indigenisation, but if we assess it by Laenui's and Enriquez's terms, perhaps it is not a decolonising move but a colonising one. Mātauranga Māori is seen to have economic benefits to the colony and is thus subsumed within current colonial and capitalist practice. Furthermore, this exploitation can be performed by Indigenous as well as non-Indigenous peoples.

Another example might be in the field of Traditional Ecological Knowledge (TEK), which draws on traditional knowledge to enhance scientific knowledge. TEK has received strong critique from Indigenous ecologists such as Leanne Betasamosake Simpson and Deborah McGregor,[65] who see TEK as a Western science colonising Indigenous knowledge. This knowledge is seen as an untapped resource that could be used for the

71

benefit of everybody – an idea that reprises the grievously problematic *terra nullius* assertion that was used in the nineteenth century to justify the theft of much Indigenous land. A *'scientia nullius'*, if you will, implies that traditional knowledge can be divorced from and considered separate from the people who grew, applied, tested, reworked, recorded, shared and own that knowledge.[66] For example, Australian honey producers recognise that 'mānuka' is a Māori word, but they argue that no one owns it, and that it is ridiculous for New Zealand to seek trademark protection for New Zealand mānuka honey. Māori used mānuka wood, bark, leaves and flowers in many ways, including for their healing properties. But this Māori-generated word and its cultural property have been declared a *terra nullius*, free for any and all to exploit.

The current waves of decolonisation and Indigenisation require us to be on special lookout for counter-forces of colonisation and to be ready to confront them. Enriquez via Laenui says that Transformation/Exploitation can also occur when supporting 'Indigenous causes within the general colonial structure' and states that this 'may become the popular political thing to do so the culture is further exploited'.[67] For example, the phrase 'dial-a-pōwhiri' is often used for a type of tokenism, when people organising an event decide that it would look good to have a Māori welcome at the beginning. Most of us who are Māori have been asked at one time or another to front or organise a welcome despite not being included in other parts of the event. (Further, local iwi are often expected to come and do these welcomes without being paid for their time.) Activities that we might think of as decolonial may thus at times be another form of colonisation. In seeking to tell the difference and assess if an act truly has a decolonising effect, it may help to ask: who benefits the most from this action? If the answer is Pākehā or the Western system, colonial exploitation is probably occurring.

Some Māori have found that within particular organisations decolonisation means them doing extra work in order to soothe or reassure well-meaning but misguided Pākehā. Puawai Cairns has written about this occurring in the museum sector: 'Decolonisation becomes just another series of extractive events and engagement which doesn't seem too dissimilar to colonisation.'[68] Her solution is to accept that some Western structures (like museums) can never be fully decolonised, and to focus instead on the Māori experience, in all its multiplicity, within them:

I want to see insightful interrogations into what decolonisation looks like to an indigenous person and an indigenous community – as declared by indigenous communities. ... But decolonisation processes will hopefully ensure that the immediate benefits of those conversations are for the community and not for the institution. That we won't continue to be spoken about in third person. This will be my version of decolonisation. Putting the people at the centre, and not the interests of the colonial machine.[69]

This is a good example of what is intended by reMāorification: something that can best be achieved through Kaupapa Māori or iwi- or hapū-centric approaches.

'New old' colonisation

Moana Jackson has written about another form of colonisation aspiring decolonisers should beware of. With the onset of neoliberalism, he says, and in our 'old Victorian Right hierarchical capitalist system … we are having to confront a new yet old colonisation that necessarily complicates the process of decolonisation'.[70] This brings to mind the Trans-Pacific Partnership Agreement (TPPA) – or the Comprehensive and Progressive Agreement for Trans-Pacific Partnership (CPTPP), as it became known. This free trade agreement was seen as an attack on state sovereignty in that it gave corporates undue influence in state affairs and on legislation.[71]

The potential for oppression from corporate hegemony looms like a dystopian spectre all around us – as with the merger of major corporations Monsanto and Bayer in 2018, for example. Oligopolies like this one threaten our food sovereignty and contribute to continued environmental degradation. Pākehā and Māori alike may find this concerning – we all enjoy the fruits of local, small- to medium-sized businesses working with the land. But Māori are particularly concerned because the government has historically negotiated overseas agreements without recourse to its Treaty partner.[72] Here are new opportunities for old styles of colonisation.

These opportunities are latent in many other spheres. Population growth and competition for resources have been frequent causes of historic boundary contestation, war and colonisation. The rise and rise of new global superpowers and hegemonies bring new threats to sovereignty. In a neoliberal world these powers are exercised in subtle ways that may include any or all of: occupation of a target country, investment in its land and infrastructure, fostering of diplomatic and trade relations, making and withdrawal of trade agreements, building of military holds in strategic places and spaces and even the reclaiming of land from oceans to do this. Economic takeover from behemoth states, wars, natural disaster (an ever-increasing threat in a climate-uncertain planet) and population shifts all threaten the world as we know it. These are phenomena that carry with them the potential for new configurations of colonisation. And then what about explorations to the Moon and Mars?

Closer to home, for further evidence of 'new old' colonisation in the context of Aotearoa, Jackson turns to education. He points out that some Māori-run charter schools may look like rangatiratanga in action, but in fact follow 'a Pakeha ideologically driven goal of educating people for the market'.[73] Education for the market and the commodification of education are also seen in the steadily increasing fees tertiary students pay for their courses and degrees – Jackson argues that they are a symptom of a more 'subtle and pervasive' form of colonisation.

Recent research has also noted a number of passive-aggressive behaviours, particularly latent and potent in Aotearoa New Zealand, that function like a new face on old colonisation. These include appeals to appeasement and compromise, 'epistemologies of ignorance', 'settler evasions' and 'settler moves to innocence'.[74] Full examination of this trend is still emerging, and space does not allow us to explore these issues in detail here, but Rebecca in the next chapter gives some examples of Pākehā anxieties that manifest in passive-aggressive colonial behaviour cloaked in decolonial equality; and Amanda in Chapter 4 discusses the effect of Pākehā backlash and how to combat microaggressions. Some 'new old' colonisations may be harder for us to spot, but are nonetheless a continuation of the old, invidious colonial project.

Disempowering decolonisation

Finally, as many theorists and activists have worried, is decolonisation a concept that *disempowers* rather than frees and transforms? Might it actually do the opposite to what its proponents seek to achieve? Graham Hingangaroa Smith has pointed out that attempts at decolonising retain a focus on the coloniser.[75] The Indigenous are implicit but ultimately invisible in such a dialectic. As the title of Ranginui Walker's celebrated book *Ka Whawhai Tonu Mātou* signifies, Māori like other colonised peoples are engaged in an ongoing struggle, but is that something we should look forward to for tamariki and mokopuna?

The questions are many and complex. If struggle is part of our identity now, should it always be? Can we call an end to the process of decolonisation while we live in a post-colonial settler state? Can Te Tiriti o Waitangi be the basis for a reinvigoration and reconfiguration of relationships, or does it inextricably bind and embed the coloniser–colonised dyad? Hokowhitu summarises the concerns:

Perhaps, then, 'decolonisation' should focus on the continued inhabitance of Indigenous consciousness by a will to resist the coloniser, whether s/he be imaginary or not. For such a dialectic is not a healthy state of mind; constant referral to the power another holds over oneself can only lead to the state where Indigenous people romanticise a pure-precolonial past, are anxiety ridden in the present dialectic, and resigned to a future where our identities will be tied to an eternal colonial struggle. As witness to the current academic discourses surrounding Indigenous resistance (underpinned by the notion of 'decolonisation'), it seems to me that the oppressed creature, in its evolution, has developed a 'holier-than-thou' self-righteousness ... who, instead of theorising and articulating their subjectivity, reverts to tears and self-pity.[76]

As the word 'imagining' in our book title suggests, we think we need to be able to dream and conceptualise our way past this dialectic, past our justified mourning, to the changes that might follow our decolonising actions. Rather than being stuck in a constant defensive crouch, we also need to be ready to accept that others may have accepted a decolonising mandate, and let our guard down so that we can work as allies. Only then might we be able to move past the framework of struggle and resistance and into a newly restored future. The final section discusses how this could look and what it might mean.

ON THE THRESHOLD

This is what decolonization means at a very practical level – taking back our power.[77]

Decolonisation is many things. It is untangling and stripping away. It is rediscovery, recovery and affirmation of a non-colonial identity. It starts in the mind, but requires action. It is taking power back. It is liberation. But once the liberation has occurred, what do we move on to?

Although not discussed in great detail here, the widespread paid and volunteer efforts to ecologically decolonise Aotearoa of rats, possums, stoats, old man's beard and other noxious exotic species may provide a helpful touchstone for considering the decolonisation of human systems. In this metaphor, we restore taonga like the bush. We cannot reverse all past harms – resurrect the trees that were felled, or bring back to life the species that were driven to extinction – but we *can* remove the destructive colonial imports so that the endemic plants and animals can thrive again. We do not seek to banish all European species from Aotearoa (you can still grow tulips and roses in your garden, for instance, or keep a carefully monitored pet cat!), but we want to ensure that those that remain do so in balance, without damaging te taiao or Indigenous ecosystems.

What does this mean for people, culture and the built environment? Let's return to the whare/house metaphor, which invites us to ask some grounded questions about the decolonisation endeavour.

- Perhaps we like the Western house the way it is and make no changes. Is that the sign of a colonised mindset? Or autonomy at work?
- Are we simply redecorating a rented house to look more like a whare? Could that be enough, for now? Or do we lose not only control but our own handiwork by embellishing the whare as tenants only?
- We gain some land and property back – not the whole neighbourhood, but some old houses and other sites to care for and build on. What do we do with them? We might restore the houses and construct new whare, reconnect with the stories in the land and the ancestors who used to live there.
- Can the above stimulate change across the entire neighbourhood and how people live?
- What systems, legislation and policy need to be addressed to support widespread change?

Perhaps decolonisation is a threshold to something else, something altogether different. That something may start with conscientisation[78] and look like what Hokowhitu calls 'Indigenous existentialism', located in the everyday and in the immediacy of an Indigenous body able to play and imagine, contingent on 'choice, freedom and responsibility'.[79] It may be about the centring of Indigenous peoples, even in Western structures, as Puawai Cairns has argued. It may be conceptualised as the restoration of the stories in this land and the rightness embedded in tikanga, as Moana will explore in Chapter 5. Or it may take on aspects of whakapapa, affirming multiple heritages and identities.

Is decolonisation a potentially divisive term for a process that leads us over the threshold to these outcomes? Is divisiveness even a bad thing if it generates a better outcome for oppressed peoples and societies? Does decolonisation just need to be better understood in the Aotearoa context? I have sought to find another way to describe the elements that people attribute to decolonisation. For me, whakapapa provides that alternative: freeing the Indigenous body to be and do as it will. As a way of working it is empowering and energising, acknowledging my pluralistic histories and identities, and giving me an imaginative platform for my actions. That may be the ultimate decolonisation, to re-theorise 'decolonisation' using an Indigenous concept.

This scenario frees up the term 'decolonisation' to become most relevant for the colonisers' descendants. These are issues that will be explored in Chapters 3 and 4, which consider that decolonisation is not just for Māori. The next chapter will ask: Why has decolonisation traditionally been seen as beneficial for Māori only? Taking the power back – crossing the threshold – may be empowering for all.

3. COLONISATION SUCKS FOR EVERYONE

REBECCA KIDDLE
(NGĀTI POROU, NGĀPUHI)

When we think about colonisation we tend to think about the ways that colonisation has affected Indigenous communities, and – as highlighted by Mike in Chapter 1 – these have been overwhelmingly negative. Yet perhaps we're overlooking something. It is possible that colonisation also impacts negatively on colonisers, on their descendants and, in the case of Aotearoa, on more recent migrants whose ancestors may not have been part of the early colonisation process.[1] What would this look like? Given that most writing on colonisation focuses on the impact of colonisation on Indigenous peoples, and that there doesn't seem to be a lot written about other impacts, we wanted to think about these issues.

I put the question to my Facebook friends – a mix of friends, family and acquaintances who identify as both Māori and Pākehā, with a number based in or hailing from overseas. 'How has colonisation impacted negatively on non-Māori?' I asked. I received answers from people belonging to all of these groups, giving examples of the negative effects colonisation has had on Pākehā New Zealanders.[2] Six strands of thought are explored below.

WHAT IS PĀKEHĀ IDENTITY?

The first group of answers suggested that colonisation had contributed to a lack of clear Pākehā identity. As researchers Awanui Te Huia and James Liu write, 'Pākehā typically report weaker ethnic identity than minorities, and often define themselves in terms of the superordinate national identity'.[3]

The narrative that the only thing that makes New Zealand unique is Māori identity and culture is a pervasive one, woven throughout our society. It leaves many Pākehā who have been born here (as perhaps their parents have, and their parents' parents) with a feeling that they lack a sense of identity.[4] Rachel Kingi, a friend from secondary school, responded to my Facebook post saying that it became evident in conversations with a Pākehā friend that her friend lamented this lack of identity and linked it to a lack of belonging and tradition. Kingi asked of Pākehā, 'What are their traditions?' She intimated that Pākehā are often proud of Aotearoa but don't feel they are part of the things that make Aotearoa special. 'They are proud of the uniqueness of Aotearoa but don't feel like they can own that.'[5]

Glenn Colquhoun, a poet, doctor and Pākehā father to Māori children, writes that 'being exposed to things Māori has usually only made me more Pākehā'. He adds, 'It makes me ask what are those things within my own culture that define me? I see things that define Māori in spiritual and cultural terms but when you are from a larger, majority culture it is sometimes harder to see yourself, there is less contrast and fewer things to say this is who I am.'[6]

Interestingly, Colquhoun notes, this often changes when Pākehā New Zealanders travel and live overseas. For the first time, they may be thrust into the position of being a minority. The new context forces Pākehā to 'start seeing themselves',[7] and they often embrace aspects of Māori culture that they would not have embraced at home. Living in the United Kingdom for seven years, this was definitely my observation. In order to exemplify their New Zealand identity many Pākehā would wear pounamu pendants and do the haka in pubs and bars whenever the All Blacks played. Te Huia and Liu write, 'In an international context, it is likely that Pākehā will utilise Māori cultural symbols as a point of distinction with the foreign host culture and other sojourners, thus creating a positive social identity partially grounded in Māori culture'.[8]

Although the project of colonisation works to overlay one identity and value set on an already existing one, it also seems to have resulted – some generations on – in many Pākehā feeling ill at ease with their cultural roots, traditions and sense of identity. When confronted with completely different cultural contexts, many look to Māori cultural identities to display their New Zealandness. Again, Glenn Colquhoun offers a useful frame through which to think about Pākehā identity:

As an immigrant culture it seems at times Pākehā are a book without a cover, one with the first chapter missing. For me, being Pākehā now is enormously exciting. It means we get a chance to write that chapter, or at least compile the stories that reveal it. Other cultures often come complete with mythologies of beginning but there do not seem to be enough celebrated stories that adequately define the journey that was to take place for us here. I think we came expecting to continue the way we always were – just in a new place. There didn't seem to be any need for explanation. We didn't expect the place to change us, to colonise us. That was our job.[9]

Colquhoun speaks of an exciting opportunity for Pākehā to build confidence in a Pākehā identity – one that sits alongside, not in combat with, Māori identities.

THE INTERGENERATIONAL TRAUMA OF THE STIFF UPPER LIP

A relative in my Pākehā family who also has Māori heritage, Rachael Marwick, suggests a possibility related to the lack of identity: that settlers, or at least the descendants of settlers, carry with them intergenerational trauma. 'There's surely residual intergenerational trauma', she says, 'associated with having left loved ones … that may have something to do with the culture of emotional reservation prevalent in older generations.'[10] Former Green Party MP Catherine Delahunty seems to agree, adding that many Pākehā descend from peoples who have been marginalised through history. This marginalisation in their original homes led many to come to New Zealand in a quest for better lives, a strident march towards material advantage that sometimes resulted in spiritual emptiness (with the latter surely having some relationship to intergenerational trauma). Few turned back to acknowledge their roots. Delahunty writes:

The Pākehā contradiction comes from our origins, so many of us being the descendants of families starved out of Ireland, burnt out of the highlands of Scotland and made surplus people in the English class system. We, the children of cannon fodder and global capitalism can barely acknowledge the loss of bones and sacred places left on the other side of the world. The severing from ancestors and from the land has brought us material advantage and spiritual emptiness. The denial of this condition assists us in our denial of the tangata whenua indigenous reality and justifies our control of resources. But it has required a weird forgetfulness.[11]

It seems that for Pākehā there may be at least three types of unacknowledged trauma that have arisen from colonisation; and, whether their ancestors were deliberately complicit or not, some of this trauma has filtered down to our current generation. First, it is traumatic for anyone to have to leave people whom they love, especially for those from a culture that is often stereotyped by its suppression of emotion. It must have been hard for their ancestors to come to Aotearoa understanding that they would likely never see their families and friends again.

Secondly, in order to get on, a semi-severing of ties to the motherland might have felt like the only option (though clearly many elements of 'Home' were brought to New Zealand to re-create a home in this new place, such as grid-city layouts, the Westminster system and roast dinners, to name a few). As Delahunty points out, perhaps something was lost along the way, and that loss continues to pervade Pākehā whānau and the Pākehā character.

Thirdly, acting as colonisers – taking part in an often racist and inherently unfair process – is surely bad for the soul of Pākehā. Being brutal can't be great for a person's ongoing sense of self (as discussed in Mike's earlier chapter). This ongoing tussle with who one is would have only been exacerbated for those who came to New Zealand to get away from a marginalising class system that didn't afford them respect or opportunity in the country they came from.

'Yeah, but all that stuff happened three generations ago – it's nothing to do with us!' I hear you cry. A recent study in the United States suggests that not only can trauma travel across generations through behavioural influences (e.g., a violent father raising a violent son), it may in fact change one's DNA.[12] Researchers found that sons (not daughters, interestingly) of Union Army soldiers who faced diabolical conditions as prisoners of war were more likely to die young than sons of soldiers who hadn't been prisoners, despite the sons having been born after the war. Epigenetic researchers believe that genes are switched on and off during times of stress and trauma and these epigenetic changes are inherited by later generations, setting diseases in motion. It seems likely that leaving a homeland and forging new lives here in Aotearoa led to stress and trauma for settlers and, though not equal to the trauma of colonised peoples, it may well have had a negative impact on their descendants. No one moves forward easily if wounds aren't healed properly. At worst, they get infected, and at best they leave a scar.

FEARFUL AND ANXIOUS PĀKEHĀ

An American friend and ex-colleague of mine, Jessica Sewell, lives in Charlottesville, Virginia (the site of the white supremacist rally in 2017 where a counter-protestor was murdered by a white supremacist who drove his car into a crowd). She argued in her response to my Facebook question that colonisation, which she equates to racism, can elicit fear in those *being* racist or *doing* the colonisation. Sewell asserts that 'Racism (and colonialism) feed on the fear of the other …. Colonizers live in fear of what [might] happen … of contamination; of difference. This brain-numbing fear is visible in the words and faces of white nationalists …'[13]

Closer to home, sociologist Avril Bell agrees that fear can breed among those exerting power over other groups, suggesting that Pākehā are often fearful of interacting with Māori on their terms. She says:

Pākehā lack of acclimatization to the Māori world means they are frequently anxious and fearful of engaging with Māori as Māori, fearful of being a minority within indigenous contexts and uncertain of their reception (will they be made welcome or not?), fearful of the exposure of their ignorance of indigenous cultural practices, discomforted by the reminder that they are not 'at home' within indigenous contexts, that they do not know things they should know as 'native' subjects, so that their own non-belonging/settler status is exposed.[14]

The problem with this, she says, is that the dynamic of fear keeps Māori and Pākehā from fruitful everyday interactions.

At one time in New Zealand history, many Pākehā held (and some still hold) the view that the country had excellent race relations, especially compared to other colonised countries. In the 1970s, leading figures in the Māori renaissance – a movement that started as protests against the loss of land but that also led to a revival of Māori cultural practices more broadly – began contesting this view, suggesting that these 'wholesome' relations were a myth. One reason that the myth had been able to take hold was that many Māori and Pākehā did not interact meaningfully with each other on a day-to-day basis – despite much intermarriage between the two groups, and government policies that tried to pepperpot or sprinkle Māori whānau throughout towns and cities, so Māori would become like Pākehā. Consequently, Pākehā society did not accept Māori culture and ways of living as being important to wider New Zealand identity and culture. Everyday interactions were – and arguably continue to be – on Pākehā terms. In everyday conversation, it was and is common to hear derogatory remarks towards Māori justified by statements like 'Some of my best friends are Māori!' Māori are still stereotypically regarded as being good 'mates' if they are happy-go-lucky, good at singing and don't 'rock the boat' – signals that these friendships are on Pākehā terms.

These one-sided interactions happen even within families. Take for example my own whānau. Not long ago, one of my brothers, my husband (a recently migrated Briton) and my Pākehā cousin entered a team into the IronMāori triathlon in Hawke's Bay. On registration, participants write their iwi affiliation or ethnicity and this goes on the name plate that you pin on to your shirt as you run and cycle. Watchers in the crowd can yell 'Go Tane from Ngāti Porou!' or simply 'Go Ngāti Porou!', whether they know you or not. My cousin had put 'Pākehā' as her ethnicity, which was noted on her name plate, while my brother had 'Ngāti Porou'. At the after-party to celebrate, on seeing my cousin and brother together with their name plates on, a Pākehā relation of ours asked accusingly of my cousin, 'Why do you have "Pākehā" under your name? Aren't we all the same?' as if to suggest that it was somehow offensive to highlight the fact that my brother and cousin were ethnically and culturally different.

That small comment was pregnant with meaning. On the face of it, wasn't my relation just asserting that we were all equal? And yet something didn't feel right. For me, it was the fact that the 'same-ing' of Māori and Pākehā both denies Māori the opportunity to celebrate their identity and culture in a society that for the most part hasn't celebrated it (except when the All Blacks play) and denies the fact that Māori lives are lived slightly differently to those of Pākehā – particularly by those who are obviously Māori. These differences might be small – the assumption that I would steal sunglasses at the local chemist but that my Pākehā cousin wouldn't, or an explicit lack of expectation from schoolteachers that I could do well academically – but they can be significant. For example, at high school when I once voiced a desire to be a lawyer, one of my teachers responded with, 'No, think about what you can do with your hands. Māori are good with their hands.'

Returning to Bell's argument above, we might decide that my relation's comment came from a place of fear or anxiety. Perhaps subconsciously they felt that acknowledging ethnic and cultural differences might mean that they would also have to acknowledge that being Pākehā is qualitatively different from being Māori. Being Pākehā means being afforded privileges that Māori have not generally received. Sometimes this privilege is hard to see when people are different within families, but the most obvious privilege is that my relation's value sets and cultural understandings are taken as the norm in most situations in New Zealand society.

Researcher and lecturer Jo Smith talks of the ways in which Pākehā obsess over national identity while being uneasy about it at the same time. She notes that 'the settler nation is deeply vexed by its own precarious identity'.[15] This obsession and unease, she goes on critically, 'constantly diverts attention and energy away from building or expressing more affirmative affinities and transformative modes of social organisation.'[16]

While it might be a privilege, one obvious downside of your worldviews always being understood by society to be 'normal' is that you are less likely to reflect, question and re-evaluate those worldviews, or be encouraged to do these things. Dominant cultures are often invisible because of the mere fact of their dominance; their thinking is ever present. But if your worldviews are never questioned, this will limit new personal experiences, thinking and innovation.

Talk to anyone who has lived overseas for a period of time and most will say that living in a context different to their own has led them to reflect on their own cultural understandings. Te Huia and Liu[17] go so far as to say that those from majority cultures tend to find it harder, and those from minority cultures easier, to cope well in new overseas cultural contexts. The latter effect is due to the fact that minority group members have had more opportunity to practise 'ethnic identity negotiation'. Ethnic identity negotiation (EIN) is a theory promulgated by Stella Ting-Toomey, who suggests that minority group members may be better skilled at intercultural relationships *because* they've had to survive in a society where they are the minority. They develop psychological resources that those of the majority group do not have, because, being the norm in that society, the majority group haven't had to engage with other cultural groups unless they so choose.[18]

Following the earlier assertions of Colquhoun, if we really *truly* want to move forward, relinquishing power and challenging 'normal' might not be so bad.[19] It may be scary but there is much for all to gain.

THE CAPITALIST AGENDA AIN'T GOOD FOR NO ONE

Capitalism is an economic system that affords people freedom to accumulate wealth. It is now generally tied to neoliberalism, an ideology or way of thinking about our economic and political system that argues for the removal of government intervention in trade, and is underpinned by the idea that private ownership is the most efficient way of managing resources and generating profits. According to neoliberal thinking, resources will be allocated by a free and unregulated market that enables competition. Neoliberal thinking has spread to most corners of the globe as the dominant, or at least a very influential, way of organising economies and politics.

As Catherine Delahunty noted in the passage I cited earlier, a quest for capital formed the basis of the colonial project. Elisapeta Heta, a friend of mine of Māori, Samoan, Tokelauan and Pākehā descent, equates capitalism with colonisation. She writes, 'Capitalism to me has always seemed like a direct branch of the colonisation tree. Individualisation to the point of fighting for survival, dividing of the haves and have-nots. Hyper materialistic mentalities ...'[20]

Others have made the same link between capitalisation and colonisation that Heta does. For example, community organiser Kassie Hartendorp in her article 'Utu and Capitalism: A Harmful Imbalance' suggests that capitalism in Aotearoa today is predicated on the suppression of Indigenous knowledge and ways of doing things.[21]

Both colonisation and capitalism focus on capturing as much and as many of the available finite resources as possible, for individual gain. The focus on the individual in colonial Western societies is borne out very clearly in land rights, for example, whereby private ownership trumps collective ownership. This way of thinking about land ownership completely flummoxed hapū and iwi, who were used to thinking of land as collectively held and cared for, for the benefit of all members of a group, including future generations. This led to confusion when colonisers 'acquired' land to on-sell to prospective settlers. Many a deal was done where collectively held land was 'sold' to Pākehā, leaving Māori thinking that they weren't giving up their rights to live on the land, but receiving payment for others to have a share of the land and to live there too. Or land was gifted by Māori for educational or religious purposes, later to be sold for a significant profit when no longer in use by government and churches.[22]

More generally, there is now much written by political theorists on the ills of capitalism, the neoliberalist form that it currently takes in New Zealand and internationally, and what that means for life in New Zealand. Take for example *The Piketty Phenomenon: New Zealand Perspectives*, a collection of essays responding to Thomas Piketty's 2013–14 book, *Capital in the Twenty-First Century*. For the most part the fourteen authors focusing on New Zealand perspectives support Piketty's thesis that current models of capitalism have led to inequality (because they are based on the false assumption that if things are left to competitive markets this will ultimately stabilise allocations of wealth and income).[23] Piketty argues that inequality has risen dramatically since the late 1970s and that this trend is likely to continue because wealth stored in capital – such as land and inheritances – grows much faster than wealth earned from income. Put simply, those who own stuff get richer more quickly than those who work for their income.

While Piketty has critics,[24] and he himself outlines the limitations of his work, his work created a stir both internationally and in Aotearoa. This would hint at the fact that many, perhaps even most of us, don't want vast inequalities to exist in our societies, particularly if those inequalities are predicated on a system that was built to profit from, and with the profits of, stolen land.[25] In the next section I discuss in more detail the idea that we New Zealanders find inequality distasteful.

Writer David Callahan outlines five key critiques of capitalism globally.[26] First, as we have seen, it produces inequality. Money makes more money, and news stories highlighting the fact that the 'globe's richest 1% own half the world's wealth' abound.[27] Secondly, capitalism is 'too unstable and prone to crisis'. Take for example the Global Financial Crisis of 2007–08, in which a full-blown banking crisis led – somewhat ironically, given neoliberalism's penchant for lack of government intervention – to government bail-outs of the failing banks. Thirdly, untrammelled capitalism depends on exploiting nature, a premise that has caused much environmental degradation and led us into this climate change mess. Next, Callahan asserts that capital has subverted democracy by hijacking government to win 'special favors', as he calls them. See, for example, the point above about government bail-outs.

Finally, he asserts that 'extreme market forces are corrupting us *as individuals* – morally and ethically'. He goes on to say that capitalism basically makes us bad people.

Plenty of progressives think and talk about the downsides of greed and materialism, along with the market's ruthless focus on efficiency, but almost always in service of concerns about economic security or ecological well-being. What you don't hear so often are these aspects of capitalism critiqued on the grounds that they make us *worse people* – less connected to family and friends, less empathetic and caring, ruder and less patient, more focused on instant gratification, less sexually responsible, more gluttonous, more misogynistic, and so on.[28]

We've already established that most of us don't want to be bad people; in fact quite the contrary, we don't want gross inequality in our society. While it is true that properly regulated capitalism *may* raise standards of living, to the benefit of many, the current neoliberal system holding sway – shaped in the image of Ruth Richardson – does not have these benefits.

The capitalist system has underpinned New Zealand's history. For the most part it has existed free from critique – with no questions asked as to the provenance of nation-building capital and about who, through the pernicious tool of colonisation, benefited most from the land-based capital (arguably the most important type of capital of all) that was dubiously acquired. Colonisation is the fraternal twin of neoliberalism: unregulated capitalism makes capitalists worse people, and colonisation makes colonisers worse people. These systems are good for no one.

INEQUALITY IS AS CORROSIVE AS RUST

Expanding on David Callahan's inequality argument, Maxine Boag – a Pākehā local government politician and family friend – asserts that our moral compass should point to a desire for equality, not for the spoils of colonisation. This equality, she argues, has broader well-being implications for the whole of New Zealand society. Boag says that

anything that enhances – or diminishes – the well-being of Māori, enhances or diminishes the well-being of our community. Health is ... not merely the absence of disease. How can we 'colonisers' experience this state [of well-being] when indigenous members of the community are marginalised, much more likely to be impoverished and unwell as they live beside us? Inequality is a corrosive force, like rust.[29]

The gap between rich and poor in Aotearoa New Zealand has widened at a staggering rate. In the 1980s and 1990s the gap widened faster than in any other developed country.[30] While the widening slowed down in the early 2000s, following the Global Financial Crisis the gap looks to be growing again.[31] These days the 'wealthiest 20 per cent of households in New Zealand hold 70 per cent of the wealth, while the top 10 per cent hold half the wealth'.[32]

Lisa Marriott and Dalice Sim in their working paper *Indicators of Inequality for Māori and Pacific People* found that between 2003 and 2013 median weekly incomes increased for all ethnicities in New Zealand, but the incomes of Europeans increased considerably more (41.2 per cent) than those of Māori (30.3 per cent) or Pacific people (5.8 per cent). Marriott and Sim state that the median weekly income gap between Māori and European populations over that ten-year period has increased 103 per cent, and between Pacific and European populations, 203 per cent.[33] Māori wealth in 2010 averaged just over $18,000, compared to $125,500 for Pākehā.[34] Only 6 per cent of New Zealand remains as Māori freehold land.[35] Māori home ownership rates have dropped 20 per cent from 1986 to 2013, to 43 per cent;[36] while the European home ownership rate dropped 11.2 per cent in the same period, from nearly 79 per cent to 70 per cent.[37] And, finally, the Māori economy is estimated to represent 6.1 per cent of the total New Zealand asset base in 2013[38] – a small proportion of New Zealand's wealth – though recent reports suggest that it is growing. In 2018, estimates put the Māori economy at $50 billion. According to an opinion piece by Joshua Hitchcock, to reach parity with our Pākehā peers it needs to grow at an even faster rate. He draws on household net worth statistics from June 2018 which note that the median net worth of a Pākehā New Zealander is $138,000, compared with a $29,000 median net worth for Māori – 'a full 79% less than that of Pākehā'.[39]

The link between subjective well-being (that is, self-reported well-being) and income is also now well established.[40] This means that with widening income gaps comes a reduction in subjective well-being in those less well-off. Boag's assertions that our own well-being rests on the well-being of others ring true when delving into the empirical evidence. A recent study has found that, in New Zealand, our individual subjective well-being seems to rest on the well-being of our wider collectives.[41] If others in the community are not doing well, we New Zealanders tend to not feel good.

THE ANSWER IS EASY PEASY: COLONISATION SQUASHES CREATIVITY

Finally, and perhaps most tragic, is the way colonisation has squashed Indigenous knowledges – and therefore eradicated creativity and mātauranga that could have contributed to solving the world's 'wicked' problems. Tina Ngata, a Ngāti

Porou friend and an environmental and Indigenous activist and writer, responded to my 'How has colonisation impacted negatively on non-Māori?' question by saying:

Easy peasy ... the world needs indigenous wisdom in order to survive and colonization suppresses it. ... consider all of the Sustainable Development Goals by the UN ... all require tools that our ancestors already utilised. Holistic thinking, connected communities, high levels of creativity ... Colonization suppresses the greatest resource for wellbeing and continuity of humankind.[42]

My husband, a migrant from the United Kingdom who works alongside Māori, Pākehā and Samoan researchers, discovered the importance of Māori knowledge in a recent research project. He and his fellow researchers were looking into the idea of social exclusion,[43] using focus groups with a range of people who experience mental distress – including a Māori group. In these groups they explored concepts of social exclusion, stigma and discrimination. The research found that Māori (and Pacific) participants challenged the mainstream response and treatment of mental distress using prescription drugs. This was due to the fact that these drugs had the potential to take away the mana (in this case meaning agency or value) of a person. These ideas challenged Western assumptions of unwellness and the framing of mental distress as disease. The research team concluded that mainstream approaches to mental distress in Aotearoa would benefit from Māori and Pacific understandings of mental illness (although, as raised by Ocean in the previous chapter, any borrowing and application of these understandings must take care not to exploit Indigenous practices or contribute further to the colonisation of knowledge). If Māori worldviews were privileged in understandings of mental health this could help undercut the negative stereotypes in the Western model and support better responses to mental illness for the wider New Zealand population.

In a 2017 interview, Noam Chomsky, one of the most cited academics in the world today, suggested in response to a question about the wicked problem of climate change and environmental decline, that Indigenous people would be the world's saviour. He said:

Anyone who's not living under a rock knows that we're facing potential environmental catastrophe and not in the distant future. All over the world, it's the indigenous communities trying to hold us back: first nations in Canada, indigenous people in Bolivia, aborigines in Australia, tribal people in India. It's phenomenal all over the world that those who we call 'primitive' are trying to save those of us who we call 'enlightened' from total disaster ...[44]

Contemporary and future problems deserve

our immediate attention with the widest set of approaches and solutions we can bring to bear. If Indigenous knowledges are disregarded, undermined by the ongoing effects of colonisation, the effects are bad for all.

And the undermining of Indigenous knowledge happens every day. In my own institution a colleague was recently in a research meeting where the discussion turned to PhD scholarships. A senior Pākehā academic asserted that applicants needed to have had overseas experience to make them viable candidates for PhD study here in New Zealand. He said he would always send good master's students overseas for doctoral study. Another Pākehā colleague responded that this view was incredibly problematic if we consider that Māori students may wish to further develop Māori knowledge in their postgraduate projects. Studying overseas would do little to support this, and be detrimental to many students. The senior academic responded, 'No, but I'm talking about students doing *science*' – the implication being that Māori knowledge was not 'real' science.

Max Harris, in a 2018 opinion piece in *E-Tangata*, asserts that 'Dismantling systems of oppression, including those based on race and class, is important for the powerful as well as the powerless'.[45] He goes on to quote the American poet and scholar Fred Moten: 'I don't need your help. I need you to recognise that this shit is killing you too, however much more softly …' Through problems of identity, intergenerational trauma, anxiety and fear, neoliberalism leading to inequality, and loss of Indigenous knowledge, powerful Pākehā and other tauiwi in Aotearoa have suffered from colonisation, softly – just as less powerful Māori have, more obviously and far less softly.

Colonisation has been good for no one.

4. PĀKEHĀ AND DOING THE WORK OF DECOLONISATION

AMANDA THOMAS (PĀKEHĀ)

Colonisation has been bad for everyone – creating an unequal and unjust society – but Pākehā have also benefited in many ways. A colonised society was created through Pākehā ideas about how things should be, so it is our responsibility as Pākehā to step back from those outdated ideas, take the cues from Māori leadership and do the work of decolonisation.

Below, I describe some of the behaviours and ideas we might challenge in our decolonisation work, and discuss the positive things we can do to build a better society. The behaviours and ideas range from overtly racist ones (what some people identify as white supremacy) through to the subtle ways that our society and economy is structured to best suit Pākehā culture (white privilege).[1] One important thing to acknowledge in decolonisation work is that, when tracing the effects of colonisation, intentions don't really matter. Some people tend to think of racism as an intentional act by an individual or group. But if we understand racism only in this way, we miss all the subtle and nuanced ways that an ethnic group might be favoured over another (this is often referred to as unconscious bias). So as well as overt behaviours and ideas, we need to look at underlying systems and processes that unfairly benefit Pākehā. For example, dominant ideas about education reflect Pākehā ideas about how things should be, to the detriment of Māori. Pākehā will naturally have a head start in such an education system.

Because of the complexity of colonisation and its effects, decolonisation is complex, highly political work. What decolonisation looks like for Pākehā and how we engage in it depends a lot on our relationships. One of the ideas we want to emphasise in this book is that Pākehā and other tauiwi should take our cue from Māori in the work of decolonisation – that means Māori set the agenda and are leaders in discussions about decolonisation. As Pākehā work towards decolonisation within our communities, it's important to constantly check back in on what Māori communities and leaders are saying and actually asking for – without expecting hand-holding or back-patting.

REFLECTING: WHY DO WE NEED TO DO DECOLONISING WORK?

As the previous chapter in this book laid out, colonisation is bad for everyone for many reasons. One of the really exciting aspects of decolonisation is that it can help Pākehā better understand who we are. In doing the work of decolonisation – developing a better understanding of the history of this place and creating a more equitable society rooted in Māoriness – Pākehā will find out more about our own histories, our own families and our own culture.

A Pākehā sense of identity is focused on connection to the land, but it's also based on actively ignoring how we came to be connected to that land (our collective history).[2] For many Pākehā, we're almost proud if we don't know who our ancestors are and how they came here. There are a number of white nationalist groups that seek to elevate British and European culture as part of their claims of white superiority, but many Pākehā are proud *not* to be European, and understand that we are culturally very different to Europeans, although we share common roots. Connections to Europe aren't seen to be important because we belong here now. But while we know where we are, and who we are not, we're not at all sure who we *are*.

My ancestors were that very generic Pākeha mix of Scottish, Irish and English. I still don't know a lot about them, but recently I've found out more about one side of my family. They came to Canterbury from Scotland, and soon after arriving bought land that had until recently belonged to Ngāi Tahu. As we know through the extensive research that went into the Ngāi Tahu settlement claim, the ways by which Pākehā came to own land involved deception, dishonesty and fundamental misunderstandings.[3] Probably my ancestors came here for economic opportunities, but they were part of broader colonising efforts to 'civilise' this place and 'tame' the land and Indigenous people. At the time, this taming and civilising wasn't typically seen as problematic. It wasn't until halfway through the twentieth century that white communities seriously reconsidered these ideas,[4] and we still haven't shed them completely.

One ancestor of mine, Arthur Turnbull, was part of the government forces that invaded Parihaka in 1881. These forces violently cleared people off their own land, raped women and killed the animals and plant life that the Parihaka economy relied on. Understanding a little more about this part of my family helps me understand how this country has been shaped, and the way my culture and identity is bound up and interwoven with Māori culture and history. It also makes me quite uncomfortable. My ancestor was not on the right side of history at Parihaka.

Many people have written about the importance of discomfort as an emotion as Pākehā work at decolonisation.[5] When we feel this discomfort, it can be bound up with shame, guilt and tension. Or discomfort can arise when Pākehā cultural dominance is challenged – for example, when we are in spaces like marae where Pākehā cultural norms are subordinate. But rather than trying to get rid of those feelings, it's useful for us to think about why we're feeling them and what they can teach us about our behaviour. Are we discomforted because we don't know how to act appropriately on a marae? That can be a useful response for encouraging us to be humble and learn, to watch how others behave and emulate their actions.

Max Harris warns against letting this discomfort drive us into white defensiveness.[6] He writes about four types of defensiveness – denial that racism exists; diversion, where attention is deflected from racism to a perceived flaw in Māori society; detriment-centring, where we focus only on deficits in Māori communities and ignore the hard work of Māori (for instance in securing land rights, or normalising Māori-centric health models); and lastly the demand to move on, that Māori should 'get over it'. Researchers Eve Tuck and K. Wayne Yang similarly explain that even those non-Indigenous people who do engage with ideas of decolonisation try to alleviate unwanted feelings (like shame and guilt) and seek out relief 'without giving up land or power or privilege, without having to change much at all'.[7]

Instead, non-Māori might embrace discomfort. Along with learning to sit with our discomfort, reflecting on Pākehā identity and processes of colonisation can be a foundation for thinking about how we might reciprocate the welcome extended by Māori and what it means to be held together within a Treaty relationship.

TRANSFORMING: WHAT DO WE NEED TO DO?

As Ocean wrote in Chapter 2, decolonisation needs to happen at many levels – in our minds and through many institutions and systems. The next part of this chapter addresses some of the things that Pākehā can work on – particularly around ideas about who we are and our relationships to Indigenous people – that might flow through from our individual behaviour into broader systems.[8]

Getting names right

As a speaker of any language, you will know that doing your best to pronounce words correctly is really important for helping people to understand what you're saying. The same goes for the Māori language. 'Kēkē' is armpit, 'keke' is cake.[9] It's an important difference.

Saying words right, especially names, is also

about respect for that person or place. My partner is a teacher and in one of his jobs he taught Māori students in their senior years of school who had *never* had their name pronounced correctly by a teacher. It made them feel disrespected.

There is a lot of patience and generosity out there for people who have a go at proper te reo pronunciation. It can be hard for English speakers to wrap their arero (tongue) around words like 'arero', but it's never too late to try. My granny is a white lady in her nineties. She's spent most of her life in one of the most Pākehā districts in Aotearoa New Zealand. I like spending time with her because she makes unexpected and hilarious jokes and she's smart. A while ago, we went for a drive together and we were chatting about a wee settlement called Motunau near her home town. My whole life I've heard it pronounced 'Mutton-now'. But Granny said it 'More-too-naa-oo', something a lot closer to the correct pronunciation. I just about stalled the car, I was so surprised.

'Granny', I asked, 'why did you say "Motunau" like that?' And she said, 'Because I think it's about time people tried to say it right.' Nau is a type of coastal grass that grows on the coast and offshore motu (islands). Pronouncing the name correctly is much more meaningful and beautiful than demanding some old sheep meat.

Listening and trusting

A fundamental aspect of decolonising work is listening to Māori and trusting what they tell us about their experiences of society – and particularly of racism. Many experiences Māori have are very different to the experiences of Pākehā, because of the Eurocentrism embedded in many of this country's systems and institutions. Learning about this is an essential first step in understanding what structures need to change and how they might change.

For example, for many Pākehā the majority of our experiences with the police are positive. We have faith in that organisation, and the people who work for it, to keep us safe and protect us. If we see a problem, the police are often who we call to report the problem and get help to fix it. However, for many Māori, interactions with the police are negative – violent even. Police in Aotearoa New Zealand don't have to record statistics about who they pull over or search, or the nature of those interactions. But research has shown that the police force is a racist institution and that Māori have good reason for their poor perceptions of the police. For instance, police are seven times more likely to use force, such as police dogs or a baton, against Māori compared to Pākehā.[10] In 1998 there was a study of Māori attitudes to police commissioned by Te Puni Kōkiri and the police.[11] One of the focus group participants, an older woman, said:

Most of my experience with the police has been through family and friends and it's not to do with any crimes, my experiences are to do with harassment and young people being searched and badly handled, and handled in a racist way. But I'm not talking about once or twice, I'm talking about every time they went out the gate.... One of [my sons'] friends [was] bashed and had to be hospitalised. She was a 25 year old university student who asked the police what her nephew had done wrong. She didn't ask in an aggressive manner. She was bashed and had to have a lot of stitches to her face and head.[12]

I know many, many Pākehā who simply wouldn't believe what this woman said. The description wouldn't match with their own interactions with the police; it would be so different to their experiences that they would ignore it or reject it as a lie or misunderstanding.

Trusting the accounts of Māori – and trying to understand the underlying factors like institutional racism that led to those experiences – is a way of acknowledging that the way Pākehā experience society is not necessarily the way that everyone else experiences it. By listening and trusting, we come to better understand that these experiences are different because of the process and ongoing nature of colonisation, in which one group (Māori) is viewed as inferior and the benefits that concentrate with another group (Pākehā) are rarely, if ever, challenged.

Pākehā are not Indigenous, and that's OK
As Bianca and Jennie explained in the Introduction, all of us involved in writing this book were also involved in the Imagining Decolonised Cities project. Part of our project was an urban design competition where people had to reimagine Porirua in a way that reflected the values of Ngāti Toa Rangatira, who are mana whenua. A video was made about one of the winning entries and this was posted on Facebook, where it quickly attracted a large number of racist comments that drew on stereotypes of Māori. Some of these comments were clearly based in white fear. One person wrote:

This pakeha isn't leaving this place. The only home I've ever known. This pakeha will not be lied about, himself or his ancestors disrespected or be made to give away anything. I am here, we pakeha are here. We are indigenous, we are not going anywhere.

This person stakes a claim to Indigeneity to ease his fears and insecurities about how exactly he fits in this place. The Standing Rock Sioux scholar and activist Vine Deloria Jr writes about encountering similar insecurities when he was the executive director of the National Congress of American Indians, telling a story about a plague of white people appearing in his office to claim an Indian grandmother. 'Why was this happening?', he asked. 'Is it because they are afraid of being classed as foreigners? ... Or is it an attempt to avoid facing the guilt they bear for the treatment of the Indians?'[13]

Deloria Jr saw white Americans scared of being labelled as foreigners, and the Facebook commenter seems to be worried about being asked to leave. But as Leonie Pihama writes, fears about being asked to leave miss the point:

I don't believe our tūpuna had an issue about sharing whenua. The issue is about control and power and who gets to determine the way we may operate as a country. We've always had embedded within te ao Māori a practice of manaakitanga.[14]

Manaakitanga involves reciprocity and demonstrating mutual respect – it is Pākehā who have not demonstrated manaakitanga.

One of the things that makes people Indigenous is that they have no other homeland to return to.[15] That means Pākehā are not Indigenous[16] – our ancestors came from somewhere else, and that place is our other homeland. But for those many, many Pākehā who see our future in Aotearoa and not back in the countries our ancestors came from, the only way to legitimise our place here is to do the work that flows from being tāngata tiriti, people who are committed to a Treaty relationship. This work involves thinking about how we came to be here, questioning relationships of power and control, and engaging in decolonisation.

Pākehā are not Indigenous or mana whenua, but that's OK.

Māori 'entitlements', entitled Pākehā: giving things up

My family did pretty nicely out of colonisation, obtaining among other things cheap land in the South Island in the 1800s. At a family birthday party I was chatting to a cousin about her university studies, and she complained about how hard it was to get a scholarship. All the scholarships were for Māori, she said. Now that I work in a university I hear this idea all the time – Pākehā students tell their Māori classmates that they only received a scholarship, or were accepted into a limited-entry class, because they're Māori.

It seems that even the small steps we have made as a society since the 1970s to redress Māori disadvantage and disempowerment – Treaty of Waitangi settlements, the setting-up of Māori institutions like kōhanga reo, wānanga and Māori TV, and yes, a limited amount of affirmative action by way of a few scholarships available only to Māori – have given rise to a sense of Pākehā grievance and claims of 'reverse discrimination'. This attitude is flatly wrong and needs to be rejected at every turn.

Funnily enough, when Pākehā repeat the idea that Māori have access to a whole lot of entitlements they don't 'deserve', they ignore all the privileges we get by the simple fact of being Pākehā. In the example of my cousin, that side of my family has inherited wealth all the way down from the ancestors who first arrived and obtained Ngāi Tahu land. This land set us up for generations; that wealth will help my cousin and me pay off our student loans, and will continue down through future generations.

Children in other Pākehā families might inherit other types of wealth. They might be bequeathed, for example, certain cultural knowledge that means they feel 'in place' and at home in universities. For the most part, our universities – essentially our whole education system – are based on Eurocentric ideas about how to teach and learn, so they 'fit' culturally for many Pākehā. This type of cultural knowledge – the right language to use, the idea that you are solely responsible for your learning and that you will mostly be measured as an individual on very confined metrics – makes university much more accessible to people who share that cultural framework, often people from Pākehā communities. It's a particular kind of privilege and resource that makes universities more accessible. Weirdly, I never had a Māori classmate tell me I was only at university because I was Pākehā and had access to a whole lot of resources that made it easier.

The example above demonstrates how access

to resources taken through colonisation has had ongoing benefits for me and my Pākehā family. It's hard to give away this sort of access once you get used to having it. Taking a more radical perspective than some decolonisation scholars, Tuck and Yang argue that non-Indigenous engagements with decolonisation have often focused on decolonising the mind only, allowing 'conscientization to stand in for the more uncomfortable [prospect] of relinquishing stolen land'.[17] In other words, to properly go through with decolonisation, non-Indigenous people will have to give up power and privilege in material ways.

There are many opportunities for Pākehā to think seriously about what is done with resources that are handed down; to consider how to support ongoing fights for Māori land to be returned (as in Waitara,[18] for example, or Ihumātao[19]); and to act on these considerations. Of course, not all Pākehā do get inheritances and my family story is very middle class, but as Rebecca wrote in the previous chapter, on average Pākehā have access to much more wealth than Māori. Beyond individual or family wealth, then, as citizens of Aotearoa New Zealand, we can advocate for better resource allocation. While we might hear a lot of complaints about Treaty settlements, to put that in perspective, the total amount spent on settlements over twenty-five years is the same as what the government spends in just two months on superannuation.[20] A broader giving up of privilege might mean non-Māori using roles within workplaces, community groups or at school to advocate for a shifting of power away from Pākehā and Pākehā norms. Often when Māori suggest change, they are overtly or subtly dismissed as angry brown people (particularly if they are women) in ways that white people are not. To challenge this kind of dismissal, and deflect some of the anger that can come when Pākehā-centrism is challenged, Pākehā can be powerful allies and workers in these battles, and use our energy and social capital to get things changed.

In many instances Pākehā don't want to get our hands dirty in these disputes because it may limit our careers and future opportunities. Many of us have children and mortgages, and insecurity is scary when you have these responsibilities. But this is where the rubber of decolonisation hits the road: Pākehā have an opportunity to get stuck in to changing institutions and organisations (always, always in conversation with our Māori colleagues and mentors – and that's important). It may be risky and unpopular, and perhaps there will be costs – in time, in financial terms, in career progression – but we need to be dogged in demanding change.

This doesn't mean, however, swooping in as 'white saviours'. We shouldn't expect thanks or reward[21] – Māori have been doing this work for decades, often without either. The reward comes through a fairer, more equitable society.

The danger of good intentions

I've been learning Māori, te reo and tikanga, for five years. I'm not very good but I love it for lots of reasons – I've made awesome friends, I've learned a lot about difference, and the language itself is poetry. My favourite word is 'heketua', the word for toilet, which means 'to go beyond'. I learn through the Ataarangi programme, and part of the Ataarangi philosophy is that the language is for everyone no matter who you are or where you're from.

Not all kura have this philosophy. Recently, I heard that teachers at one of the immersion courses I've attended a few times have been starting to worry about the tsunami of Pākehā reo Māori learners wanting to attend. There has been huge recent interest from diverse communities in learning the language. This is great in so many ways – te reo Māori is a language from this place that tells us *about* this place, and about people from here, and it helps non-Māori gain some insight into Māori worldviews.

I don't think resistance to the Pākehā students attending the immersion courses came from a general position against Pākehā reo learners. But where there are limited courses, resources and teachers available, Māori may be squeezed out. There are well-documented socio-economic disparities between Māori and Pākehā, so it's very possible that it's easier for Pākehā to take time off work, pay registration fees and travel to courses. And most Pākehā learners can step into this learning space without feeling or understanding the trauma of language dispossession[22] – after leaving class, we go back to our white, English-speaking families. Because of ignorance of our own histories, many of us don't know the languages or dialects our ancestors might have originally spoken (Gaelic, Cornish) so there's no sense of loss or anger about why we speak only English. We get to go home and be comfortable. All of this possibly denies some Māori a place on a limited-entry course to learn their own language.

I chatted about the politics of Pākehā going to these events with some of my friends. Many of them argued that we need to build a community of reo speakers, and that Pākehā are needed for this and to be advocates for the language. But Pākehā good intentions aren't enough if we don't think very carefully and deeply about the politics and power relations involved.

As growing numbers of Pākehā engage with the reo and learning about tikanga, we need to be aware that these are political processes. Pākehā should be exceptionally careful about positioning ourselves as experts in any of these spaces, think carefully about our motivations to be involved in the first place, and our capacity to navigate this with care. For some Māori, hearing Pākehā speak their language evokes feelings of shame that they themselves cannot speak the language that is their birthright. You might be a strong Pākehā advocate of the reo, but if you don't think carefully about your position as Pākehā in this space, you risk doing more harm than good by reinforcing feelings of shame or trauma.

I see this among my friends and know I've done it too – become caught up in practising what I can say at the expense of listening and reading the room. Pākehā need to proceed with humbleness and care and maintain that attitude – even when we're getting excited about the beauty of the language and how awesome it feels the first time you successfully tell a gag in the reo.

And, sometimes, spaces or resources are just for Māori. Māori need the freedom to discuss issues related to their communities without having to worry about Pākehā perceptions and emotions, and this is something non-Māori must respect.[23]

Remembering to be careful, humble and respectful around how we use the gift of te reo Māori is a lesson we can apply to other occasions when we are invited to share in Māori ways of doing things, whether this is a weaving lesson, a pōwhiri at school or work, an overnight stay on a marae or a visit to a kapa haka festival. We may embrace these experiences with good intentions – but good intentions aren't enough unless they are backed with respect and care, and an understanding of the broader structures and systems that perpetuate colonialism.

There are other things Pākehā might do to support te reo Māori, like educating ourselves about different political parties' policies on supporting the reo, and voting and donating accordingly; supporting events for Mahuru Māori and Te Wiki o Te Reo Māori; and helping to restore Māori place names by discussing with mana whenua opportunities for renaming streets and other places in our neighbourhoods.

Speaking up

Recently there's been a rise in 'call-out culture', in which exclusionary or discriminatory actions are named and the people responsible made accountable in the interests of social justice. Speaking up is necessary work – it's important to speak out against racist jokes, or transphobia, or someone who constantly speaks over women or people of colour. When white nationalists tried to march on Parliament grounds in October 2017, some of the authors in this book protested against them as a way of clearly demonstrating that those ideas were not welcome here. Free speech is an important principle, but it's not absolute. Some ideas – like white supremacy, anti-Semitism or that women belong in the kitchen – are just not acceptable in Aotearoa New Zealand, so we shouldn't entertain them. Those ideas have been found lacking – they ignore other rights that people have and lead to exclusion and hatred. We don't need to revisit them. Liberal democracy is always about balancing individual freedoms (the liberal part) with collective responsibilities (democracy). Focusing only on individual free speech ignores the 'democracy' part of the political system.

Public protests with like-minded friends are one thing, but in other situations when I hear or see racism and microaggressions, I find it really tricky to think on my feet and respond appropriately. In daily life, without the solidarity that comes from a group of fellow protestors, sometimes it is hard to feel brave enough to speak up (especially when I may not be the most senior or powerful person in the room). Below is a list of comments you might hear from non-Māori and some ideas for what you could say in response. It can be awkward to confront someone directly, and sometimes people haven't thought about this stuff before, so it's not always helpful to say flat-out, 'Hey, that's racist.' In this situation you might want to open a door rather than shaming the perpetrator.

It's also important that we think about calling out in nuanced ways. Sometimes call-out culture becomes exclusionary in itself, rather than an invitation to dialogue. If we are too harsh, or act holier-than-thou, we risk people feeling resentful of decolonisation movements rather than being supported to think and act towards a decolonised Aotearoa. I think back to my granny. When we talk politics, I engage gently. I don't want her to feel shame and I don't want to disrespect her (in fact, I know I have a lot to learn from her). It's OK to be hard sometimes and soft at other times,[24] and it's OK to be imperfect.[25] In this work, we need to avoid the tendency to tear each other down or be earnest or righteous.[26] The options below are constructive ways of inviting friends and family to take a different perspective.[27]

If someone says:
'The Māori language is dying, no one speaks it overseas, and it's a waste of time learning it.'

You might say:
'There are many reasons why someone would learn te reo. It's a beautiful, poetic language and is a joy to learn.'

'Learning te reo is a really important way of learning about Māori worldviews and getting a range of perspectives about how the world fits together.'

'The language is unique to this place – we have a responsibility but also an awesome opportunity to be part of sustaining it, and keeping it healthy.'

'Pākehā laws and rules have been hugely damaging to te reo and its speakers over time (for example, the 1867 Native Schools Act that set up schools in Māori communities but required tuition to be in English).[28] We don't need to wallow around in guilt, but trying to correct what we know was really damaging is just the right thing to do. Don't you think?'

If someone says:

'It's time that Māori moved on, the past is the past.'

You might say:

'Past harms have ongoing effects and these harms haven't been put right. Ngāi Tahu lost a huge amount of land, and things promised to them, like land for reserves, were never delivered. Yes, they've gone through a settlement process, but resources returned to them (or bought back!) are a drop in the ocean compared to what was lost. It's not hard to see how if you lost pretty much all your economic resources how difficult it is to "bounce back" from this, and the impacts it would have on your community. So let's keep talking about and working at ways that we can make this right.'

'Wouldn't it be great if all the harm was in the

past! But we know that racism is ongoing, and our institutions are still based on colonialism. So we need to fix those things. For example, regardless of the category of offence, Māori are more likely than non-Māori to be sent to prison.[29] And then the justice system itself is based on a whole lot of assumptions about what is normal and right. Maybe jails were and are normal in England, but jails didn't exist for Māori pre-colonisation.'

If someone says:

'Hēmi is only in our law/med class because he's Māori.'

You might say:

'Gosh, I'm so glad Hēmi is in our class because he brings awesome perspectives that I love hearing about. The legal/medical profession will be lucky to have him.'

'Having more diverse classes really helps me understand the world and how people can have very different experiences of medicine/the law to my own. I think more diversity is going to make me a better doctor/lawyer too, because I can see different perspectives now.'

'Māori are underrepresented in law/medicine professions. I think we need to fix that. Changing the ways students are evaluated and included at uni to encourage Māori participation is a good thing. Low Māori participation often reflects the barriers Pākehā society has created (for example the sidelining of Māori knowledge and norms, like rongoā and tikanga Māori). Adjusted requirements for Māori is one way that we can challenge these barriers.'

If your colleague sits on a table that's used for eating. (This happened at my workplace recently and I froze, feeling awkward, and did nothing. Next time I'll be better prepared!)

You might say:

'Hey, Terry, let me get you a chair. No, you're fine sitting there? Well, I think I would be more comfortable if you sat on a chair. It's not really appropriate to sit on a table because your bum is on something that food is served from. Bums and food don't mix – it's not really hygienic. I know you don't want to offend anyone or make them uncomfortable, so here's your chair. Thanks, Terry.'

If your friend is going boating on the lake, and says they're really looking forward to going to 'Ta-ow-po'.

You might say:

'Oh, Taupō! I love Taupō but I haven't been to Taupō for ages. Last time I was in Taupō, I got some delicious sushi. Hey, drive safe to Taupō.'

Your dad shares an opinion piece with you that says uninviting a white nationalist group from a campus speaking event is impinging on free speech.

You might say:

'Free speech is a great ideal, Dad – it's a really important part of our society. But we need to use it carefully. Sometimes people use "free speech" to defend hate speech. And sometimes it impinges on peoples' other freedoms or their safety. I think you and I both agree that violence targeting Muslims, for example, is completely unacceptable, so why should fascists be able to advocate these ideas in words without people telling them to shut up because their ideas are terrible and violent? Rights are paired with responsibilities.'

If a little thought creeps into your head that your friend who got arts funding targeted at Māori isn't really Māori; he's not connected to his iwi, knows nothing about Māori culture and doesn't speak the reo.

You might say to yourself:

Perhaps he is exactly the sort of person the funding is right for – maybe it will be an avenue of reconnection. But more importantly, it's not the job of non-Māori to police the identity of Māori. There's a long history of non-Māori trying to set the standard of what Māori need to do or be to be authentic. It's not our place.

CONCLUDING THOUGHTS

There's no easy answer to some of these questions about what to do, how to be a good ally or accomplice, and how to avoid our good intentions getting in the way of good decolonisation. We might want decolonisation to hurry up, but sometimes we need to slow down and make sure we proceed in a considerate way. Through good relationships within our communities, we can talk about how to approach some of these challenges, how to address them as a collective and how to be led by Māori. Having these tricky conversations respectfully will remind us to be humble in our engagements. This kind of approach means being inclusive and generous to ourselves and to others.

The mahi of decolonisation, and figuring out how we fit together in this place, will require a long-term commitment. It's a commitment we need to make to Māori – but also to each other – to listen, think and then act to create a fairer, more just society. At its base, decolonisation means Pākehā giving up some power – particularly the power of deciding what our country should look like and how it should be organised, to the exclusion of Māori visions, dreamings and restorations. This is going to mean discomfort for us non-Māori. Do we have the courage to give up power and get uncomfortable in the interests of a stronger, fairer, healthier society?[30] I think we do.

5. WHERE TO NEXT? DECOLONISATION AND THE STORIES IN THE LAND

MOANA JACKSON
(NGĀTI KAHUNGUNU, RONGOMAIWAHINE, NGĀTI POROU)

Colonisation has always been a many rendered thing. Since the beginning of the European dispossession of the world's Indigenous peoples, the colonisers have defined and redefined it in a vast story archive.

Although in the simplest sense colonisation is the violent denial of the right of Indigenous peoples to continue governing themselves in their own lands, the colonisers have told stories that redefine its causes and costs. The fact that colonisation necessarily involved the brutal taking of Indigenous peoples' lands and lives has also been reframed and justified in stories that range from pseudo-scientific and legal rationalisations to blatantly racist presumptions.

Today there are new stories. Colonisation is a *process* of dispossession and control rather than a historical artefact, and now it takes on new forms. These forms may be less obviously violent, but they still deny Indigenous peoples the right to be fully free in their own lands.

Yet many stories of colonisation are written in a stubborn past tense. They are often academic texts, filled with post-colonial rhetoric or revisionist histories that sometimes admit its past genocidal effects. Some record a detached disquiet and expressions of regret, but they often also seem to be a plea in mitigation, or try to claim that simply naming colonisation as a past wrong is somehow a defence.

If a story does acknowledge any mistreatment or contemporary disadvantage of Indigenous peoples, it usually speaks of the legacy of colonisation rather than its ongoing presence. It may victim-blame, or identify racism as a possible cause of the disadvantage, without acknowledging that racism as an ideology and practice was invented and refined in colonisation.

Indigenous peoples have spoken back against such stories but they remain the dominant narrative. Since the struggles after the Second World War of Indigenous peoples in Africa, Asia and elsewhere to reclaim their independence and self-determination, the colonisers have tried to control the meaning of decolonisation in a different story archive. They require Indigenous peoples to continue to speak the truth of their own power to the stories which the colonising states continue to tell.

Although in its simplest sense decolonisation is the reclaiming of the right of Indigenous peoples to once again govern themselves in their own lands, it has been recorded in stories that limit its meaning. The stories never allowed that the rallying cries for freedom from colonisation would apply to all Indigenous peoples who had been dispossessed. Instead they defined decolonisation as a right reserved only for those who had remained the majority population in their own countries.

Under the 'blue water' doctrine, the right to decolonise was restricted to Indigenous peoples whose lands were being governed from afar by colonisers back in the 'home country', separated by a stretch of ocean.[1] The countries where the colonisers stayed, established a government and became the majority were redefined as 'scttlcr colonies' and the Indigenous peoples were excluded from any possibility of decolonisation.

Indigenous peoples in affected 'settler colonies' such as Australia, Canada and New Zealand have always spoken back against that story too. Yet it is still the decolonising story told by the governments in those countries, even though there is an inherent injustice in restricting the basic human right of self-determination only to certain humans.

It is surely timely and just to reframe the decolonisation story so that Māori and other Indigenous peoples in the 'settler states' might also be self-determining. In this country, the potential exists to develop a different and unique decolonisation discourse because there are already stories which express the power of a different truth.

These stories reflect the hopes that iwi and hapū placed in Te Tiriti o Waitangi and they offer the chance to enhance the dignity of everyone who lives here. They do not require some false blue water dichotomy or distinctions in human rights and worth created by someone else. They are stories in this land.

If people care to listen, such stories still seep through the land. Many of them were first told and learned in the long centuries when Māori became iwi and hapū, and long before those who were called the rerekē or 'different ones' arrived on these shores. They are stories from non-colonising times. The values and hopes they contain for this land can provide the basis for a non-colonising future.

From the moment that the ancestors began to

know this land as the Mother, Papatūānuku, stories have had the capacity to guide and teach as well as entertain or warn. In the earliest stories there are lessons about how iwi and hapū became the 'we' that is tangata whenua, and how they established whakapapa as the source of relationships and knowledge. The stories were sometimes told by those whose times have otherwise barely been remembered in the passing. Together they merged into what writer and academic Rarawa Kohere has called a distinctive 'tūrangawaewae of thought'.[2]

The stories named our right to stand in this place and provided an intellectual tradition that gave us insight into the obligations that went with the right to stand. In a very real sense, they were stories of identity and home – 'home' being a concept that Jean Riki has described as the quizzical yet inexpressible joy of belonging:

Home is where the heart is
home is where the heart
home is where the
home is where?
Home is
home.[3]

The stories are also notable because they are stories of being at home on islands in the Pacific. The tīpuna never forgot that, as much as whakapapa tied us to this land, it also tied us to the Pacific Ocean that we call Te Moana-nui-a-Kiwa. When

Māui dragged the land from the sea, these islands were known as 'te tiritiri o te moana', the gift from the sea, and so they have remained.

We also used the name Aotearoa because the islands were bigger than others we may have once known. Yet we never lost sight of the fact that we were still standing on Pacific Islands and that the relationships in such a place would always be mediated through a palpable sense of intimate distance.

The beaches stretched further than any we had seen before, but they were still not as long as the far blue paths we took to get here. The broad plains gave Papatūānuku a wide and chilling face in the winter, but they never put the mountains beyond our reach. Indeed, the mountains became touchstones of our right to stand, monuments of belonging that every iwi and hapū recorded in pepeha and waiata.

Wherever we went history and the soft hands of the land kept us close. Distance was only as relative as the deep pause between sleeping and waking, and even the swirling mass of Te Kore that hung beyond the stars was only a mystery we could tell in stories where the horizon pulled at the changing tides. The night might sometimes be a long restlessness till dawn, but light still shone clear to the whatihua, the far universe where origins were forged and new thoughts flourished.

So while we learned to be at home and wondered what Papatūānuku might have to say, we developed an intellectual tradition in which the world around us was as ordinary and extraordinary as tapu. In its cleansing waters we learned that time and relationships moved with each other across the land like a river finding the sea. Whakapapa became a series of never-ending beginnings where the nature and effect of relationships crossed from the past into the future, through what Patricia Grace has called the 'now-time'.[4]

In that intimacy of time and knowledge and place, that sense of big-yet-small islandness, we lived the very human lives of people seeking the consolations and winds of home – the hau kāinga. Rather like the reassurance that is captured in Arapera Kaa Blank's memories of the Waiapu, home was a 'soul place binding bones'.

Thus we are inheritors
of interwoven dreams,
whose paua-shimmering music ever
echoes on the wind.[5]

In this intellectual tradition we learned that memory and hope may sometimes seem fanciful but they can also lead to new realities. We learned of our very human fallibility, and understood that, when conflict arose or relationships were damaged, resolution would need to be found. Like all cultures, we therefore developed a jural tradition or tikanga, which Ani Mikaere has described as the 'first law of Aotearoa'.[6]

In simple terms tikanga is a values system about what 'ought to be' that helped us sustain relationships, and whaka-tika or restore them when they were damaged. It is a relational law based on an ethic of restoration that seeks balance in all relationships, including the primal relationship of love for and with Papatūānuku. Because she is the Mother, we did not live under the law but rather lived with it, just as we lived with her.

As we grew with the law and stories in the land, each iwi and hapū became a polity bound by constitutional and political norms as well as by ties of whakapapa. These two strands were in fact inseparable. The political power of mana or tino rangatiratanga became the art of recognising the interdependence of relationships, while preserving the independence of each iwi and hapū polity.

When we drew political borders, they conformed to the contours in the land because that is where the interdependence began. They marked the possibility of movement back and forth, constrained only by recognition of the relationships others might already have with the land. Like any human construct they could be ruptured in a dispute, but resolution always followed because in whakapapa no relationship is ever beyond repair.

The ethic of restoration moved with the borders too. It was part political judgement and partly an expression of aroha – only through mutual respect and affection could balance and whakapapa be maintained.

The philosophies of our law and political power were also inseparable from the questions we asked about life itself: what is the relationship between people and the power of the land and the universe? Where do the interests of the individual fit within the well-being of the collective? How can the land and its relationships be protected in encounters with those who might have a different whakapapa and a different sense of mana and tapu?

Sometimes the answers were found in more stories, because parable and reason often serve the same ends. At other times they were reaffirmed in rituals where the ideal of what ought to be merged with everyday practice.

Thus the pōwhiri to welcome manuhiri on to the marae became a tikanga story of border crossings between the distance of visitors and the bringing together of known or hoped-for relationships. On the marae the borders were metaphorical, but we knew what they were, and we developed marae kawa as a means of ensuring that the relationships within them were just or tika.

The first voice of the karanga linked the mana of the hau kāinga to the whakapapa and possibility of relationship with the manuhiri. The karanga by the manuhiri in response was a statement of their mana, and an acknowledgement that the whakapapa and authority of the marae would be respected.

Any grief or politics of nostalgia or discontent could then be laid down in the whaikōrero with the reassurance that the jurisdiction of the marae was being accepted and the mana of the relationships was being preserved. When the distance between the people was finally closed with the shared breath of the hongi, the borders faded away in a confirmation of the relationships and the reciprocity of aroha.

In the intimate politics of those relationships, new and old stories could then be told. Treaty-making was often included in such stories because it has always been part of the political and diplomatic process. In Ngāti Kahungunu the process is called mahi tūhono, the work that brings people together. To treat is to honourably seek or mend relationships.

To be a mokopuna of an iwi or hapū was to know the stories in the land. Whether they were about heroes traversing imagined worlds or the complexities of knowledge passed on in the mind-fields of a whare wānanga, they were part of an archive of belonging that was never far away:

where the mountain meets the sky
stone of green turns gold ...
there's a story there

lonely river rushes to the sea
there's a story there.[7]

When the different ones came, they were moving into the law for our land and the land of our stories. They were also coming into our home and on to our collective marae. Certain borders had to be crossed and certain kawa laid down so that a relationship might be established.

But the newcomers came as colonisers. They had a different story to tell, and they had a different view about treaties as well as of relationships and the land.

In the nearly four hundred years that European states had been dispossessing other Indigenous peoples, the only relationships they knew were ones in which they would rule over peoples they decided were racially inferior. The only meaning they gave to the land was as property which they should own.

Those stories did not change when they arrived here. James Cook's belief that he could take this country for England in 1769 because he had 'discovered' it, and the whole discourse in the 1830s about how the Crown should 'annex' and treat with us, were based on their assumed right to take over the homes of any Indigenous peoples whom one writer would later call 'your new-caught sullen peoples / Half devil and half child'.[8]

Initially iwi and hapū were not aware that the

different ones would believe such stories and looked to the marae to decide what kind of relationship might be possible. Thus the 1835 Declaration of Independence or He Whakaputanga stressed the self-determination of iwi and hapū but allowed the kind of interdependence with newcomers that is recognised on the marae.

Five years later, when iwi and hapū first discussed whether to treat with the Crown, it was on the basis that the stories in the land could be translated into Te Tiriti as a way to bring people together – mahi tūhono. Like the kawa on the marae, the kawa of Te Tiriti envisaged the cementing of relationships that recognised the facts of iwi independence and the hopes for an inherent interdependence.

The words in the reo in Te Tiriti were an expression of that tikanga-based recognition and were signed by the rangatira on that basis. They reaffirmed that while interdependence was an honourable aim, it was always dependent upon the continuing independence of iwi and hapū. To contemplate forfeiting that independence would have been legally impossible, politically untenable and culturally incomprehensible.

Colonisation had no time for the niceties of tikanga. It fractured the hoped-for interdependence and denied the possibility of continuing Māori independence. The colonisers' need to impose their laws and institutions on people who already had their own allowed no room for an honourable relationship with iwi and hapū. Instead colonisation fomented injustice: a systemic privileging of the Crown and a relationship in which it assumed it would be the sole and supreme authority.

As they set about ensuring their supremacy through war and all the other brutality of dispossession, the colonisers wrote new stories that deliberately misremembered and obscured the injustice of what they were doing. History became a kind of rebranding in which colonisation was not seen as a violent home invasion but a grand if sometimes flawed adventure that was somehow 'better' here than anywhere else because of the proclaimed honour of the Crown in treaty-making.

There is a stark contradiction in terms in the belief that there can be honour in the dishonour of dispossession, and so the new stories never found an easy place in this land. Rather, they sat uneasily upon it like the new place names and fences that were being strung across the new private properties. They were intruder stories on a land that needed no such embellishment.

These colonial stories may have helped explain the taking of power, but they could not give the colonisers the comfort of a place to stand. It was hard to feel at home when the descendants of those who had been killed were never far away and the smoke of the battlefield still lingered in the smoke of the forests that were being burned. In island stories, the intimacy of distance never lets memory entirely fade away.

Other stories had to be told in which colonisation became a wayward and uncertain search for identity. It was often easier just to continue looking back to England as 'home' and to turn the valleys and forests and mountains of this land into a landscape that the colonisers could frame and try to keep at a distance even as they took its wealth.

But time gave security if not comfort and eventually the colonisers morphed into settlers and then 'Kiwis'. They still saw the land as a better Britain in the Pacific, but they increasingly claimed a certain permanence – while turning away from the fact that in settling themselves they were continually unsettling us.

With each new story and each new consolidation of power the colonisers took less care to listen to the stories that were already in the land. Instead they ignored them, or redefined them for their own purposes. Just as they ploughed their claims into Papatūānuku, so they ploughed old stories into new and damaging redefinitions.

Ownership redefined the tikanga of iwi and hapū relationships with the land, and sexism disrupted the complementary roles of Māori men and women. Racism reduced us to a warrior race or a compliant if noble savage, and arrogance turned sacred and complex understandings of the world into simple myths and legends. The retellings contained little of our truths, instead expressing the coloniser's belief in our inferiority: 'Uncivilised folk, such as our Māori, may not do any great amount of thinking.'[9]

In these times of loss and dying, the hope of our independence seemed to fade. The possibility of even an equitable and interdependent relationship with the colonisers receded like the mountains we could no longer touch. People sometimes lost faith in who we once were and might still be, and grew silent with the stories. Yet as the fiercely asserted right of self-determination became a selflessly determined will to survive, the old stories were told in the quiet of the marae. Old memories and histories were sung for those who would come after, and the joy of resilience provided comfort as new challenges were faced.

So the stories survived. Just as adaptation to the pressures of colonisation never meant total submission to its presumed power, so the break in the stories' telling never meant their disappearance or the destruction of the values they contained. They now speak of a defiant resolve that we will never be silent again, and of the certainty that, as whakapapa carries the past through the now-time, justice will re-emerge in the relationship offered through Te Tiriti.

Unfortunately, in colonisation's current neoliberal form the stories are being co-opted and redefined once again. These co-opted versions are used to further Crown interests – often as a clip-on perspective to its narratives of cultural respect and responsiveness. Too often these stories are removed from their historical and political beginnings and become a cultural garnish or a concert performance, rather than an expression of the independent power and integrity within which they are meant to exist.

However, enough of them are intact. Furrowed into the whakapapa, they can still call up hope even when everything might seem lost in poverty or despair. They speak of love for the land and the ties even a lost mokopuna in the city can have with a distant mountain or river. They provide reassurance that there will always be a place to stand.

Their permanence and values are a reminder that even the greatest injustice need not destroy hope. Colonisation is an injustice that is often too painful to be fully told; and the relationships it has damaged and continues to damage can seem beyond repair. Yet the stories and their hope may be a guide to resolution.

They may in fact allow a different way of thinking about how to ease the hurt and hara that colonisation causes. For, above all else, they show that remedy will best come from the ineffable hopes in this land and from the people who wish to live with it.

'Decolonisation' may not be the most appropriate word for that kind of remedy because, like colonisation, it came from somewhere else. Perhaps it could be replaced with the ethic of restoration. The use of this term would seek to replace colonisation not by merely deconstructing or culturally sensitising the attitudes and power structures that it has established, but by restoring a kawa that allows for balanced relationships based on the need for iwi and hapū independence upon which any meaningful interdependence must rest.

Such an ethic derives from the lessons in the stories in the land about the potential to whaka-tika or to make right even the most egregious wrong, and to then whaka-papa, or build new relationships. To adapt it as a tool to create non-colonising relationships is to rekindle faith in the 'ought to be' in this land; to draw upon the same land- and tikanga-centred way of ordering society that was envisaged in Te Tiriti.

Restoration (like colonisation) is also a process, not an event, and it will require a change of mind and heart as much as a change of structure. There will of course be difficulties: such transformations must confront the implacability of a power unjustly taken. It will require courageous wisdom to change, and some will say it is impossible and unrealistic. But when the ancestors crossed Te Moana-nui-a-Kiwa, they overcame what seemed impossible and realised that courage is simply the deep breath you take before a new beginning.

And there has always been another intellectual tradition in this land which cherishes different values and defines the concepts of power and democracy in a different way. There has also always been more than one way of making a nation, and Te Tiriti only ever saw a relational nation in which politics was never just the art of the possible but the promise of reconciling difference across what was only ever meant to be an intimate distance.

At one level the practical steps involved in this envisioned ethic are necessarily political and constitutional because decolonisation cannot occur within the systems and institutions which colonisation has established. The restoration of place in a non-colonising future can only be assured with the recognition and effective exercise of iwi and hapū self-determination – not as a structural subset of colonising government structures, but as the basis of constitutionally independent polities.

The right to self-determination asserted by majority Indigenous populations in other countries is also the right of Māori. Human rights are never dependent on numbers but inhere in a person's humanity.

Māori people have discussed the need for a different constitutional arrangement ever since it became apparent that Te Tiriti was being dishonoured by the Crown. The formation of the Kīngitanga in the 1860s and the establishment of the Māori Parliament in 1892 are just two examples of that desire for change.

The recent Matike Mai programme of nation-wide discussions about constitutional transformation built upon those initiatives. It was established in 2010 by the Iwi Chairs Forum with a brief given to a representative Working Group to develop new constitutional models based upon tikanga, He Whakaputanga and Te Tiriti.

More than 5,000 Māori participated in the various hui held between 2012 and 2015 and discussed a number of different constitutional 'houses' or models based upon the constitutional importance of iwi and hapū independence. The discussions were always drawn from Te Tiriti and assumed that if the Crown was to finally honour the interdependence promised within it then the terms of iwi and hapū political authority had to be acknowledged.

But the kōrero also focused on the values which

might underpin the models. In doing so they were drawing from the stories in the land. For example, all of the values they identified were based on relationships. In particular they recognised the need to re-place Papatūānuku at the centre of all political and personal relationships. To rehonour the responsibilities of a mokopuna to the earth is especially important in the current crisis of climate change.

Although the values were discussed as prerequisites for constitutional transformation they may also be seen as interrelated parts of a wider ethic of restoration.

1. *The value of place* – the need to promote good relationships with and ensure the protection of Papatūānuku.
2. *The value of tikanga* – the core ideals that describe the 'ought to be' of living in Aotearoa and the particular place of Māori within that tikanga.
3. *The value of community* – the need to facilitate good relationships between all peoples.
4. *The value of belonging* – the need for everyone to have a sense of belonging.
5. *The value of balance* – the need to maintain harmony in all relationships, including in the exercise of constitutional authority.
6. *The value of conciliation* – the need to guarantee a conciliatory and consensual democracy.[10]

Together the values reflect what Max Harris and Philip McKibbin call the 'politics of love', in which love is seen as both critical and constructive.

The politics of love is a values-based politics, which affirms the importance of people and extends beyond us to non-human animals and the environment ... it holds that all people are important – and as such it incorporates a commitment to radical equality.[11]

Constitutional transformation is only one way in which the ethic of restoration may be achieved. The earlier chapters in this volume have outlined a number of other ways in which individuals and communities can work towards the same goal. The writers are aware that change will require long-term social and economic as well as political and attitudinal transformation, but they also have confidence that such change is both necessary and possible.

Martin Luther King Jr often said, 'the arc of the moral universe is long, but it bends towards justice'. It may take a while, but with stories anything is possible. They can even shift time – it simply takes belief. As the Cherokee writer Thomas King has said: 'The truth about stories is that that's all we are.'[12]

Ben Okri has noted that rescuing the truth from old stories in order to make new understandings is essential if a country is to be all that it can be.

> Nations and people are largely the stories they feed themselves. If they tell themselves stories that are lies, they will suffer the future consequences of those lies. If they tell themselves stories that face their own truths, they will free their histories for future flowerings.[13]

Because whakapapa traverses time between the past, present and future, the building of new relationships and the telling of new stories begins with the identification and 'un-telling' of colonisation's past and present lies. Stories for and about transformation rely on honesty about the misremembered stories and the foresight to see where different stories might lead.

That is the ethic of restoration. It offers the chance, or challenge, to clutch truth and justice for 'future flowerings'.

It is concerned with the balance of relationships rather than a will to limit what they might be. And in giving back to Māori the right of self-determination, it offers everyone a place to stand – giving substance to the insight of the poet Allen Curnow that such a place could be found:

Not I, some child, born in a marvellous year,
Will learn the trick of standing upright here.[14]

Such standing comes with the reassurance of Te Tiriti. Many people find comfort in that, and it is never too late to journey towards a tikanga-based future. Witi Ihimaera, too, encourages us to start right away, in the now-time:

It's our watch now
The time to make dreams come true
Today is a good day to begin ...[15]

NOTES

Introduction

1   The Public Works Act 1864 was one of the many legislative vehicles used to alienate Māori from their land. It meant that the government could take land from Māori ownership for roads and railways and other purposes, for little or no compensation. Often the land was never used for the ostensible purpose for which it was taken – nor offered back to the original owners, as was supposed to happen.

2   The project included an urban design competition to imagine a transformed public space in Porirua City, and a day-long public hui discussing what a decolonised city could look like. See the Imagining Decolonised Cities website for more information and to view the competition entries: www.idcities.co.nz

3   'Scotty Morrison Explains Meaning of Word Pākehā after It Was Labelled a Racist Term', One News Now, 6 May 2019, www.tvnz.co.nz/one-news/new-zealand/scotty-morrison-explains-meaning-word-p-keh-after-labelled-racist-term (accessed 15 May 2019). See also Branko Marcetic, 'A History of Outrage over the Word "Pākehā"', The Spinoff, 3 March 2018, https://thespinoff.co.nz/atea/03-03-2018/a-history-of-outrage-over-the-word-pakeha/ (accessed 29 August 2019).

4   There are many good Māori dictionaries out there, but the online *Te Aka Māori–English, English–Māori Dictionary* is especially handy: https://maoridictionary.co.nz/

Chapter 1

1   'Oranga Tamariki Sees Increasing Number of Child Removals over "Systemic Racism" – Researcher', One News Now, 10 May 2019, www.tvnz.co.nz/one-news/new-zealand/oranga-tamariki-sees-increasing-number-child-removals-over-systemic-racism-researcher (accessed 29 August 2019).

2   Emma Vere-Jones quoted in Phil Taylor, 'Anti-Māori Pamphlet Shows Gaps in Hate Speech Law: Andrew Little Calls for Action', *New Zealand Herald*, 14 April 2019, www.nzherald.co.nz/

nz/news/article.cfm?c_id=1&objectid=12221767 (accessed 1 May 2019).

3   See for example the group Hobson's Pledge, which aims to remove laws and practices that address historical injustices to Māori, claiming they are discriminatory.

4   Moana Jackson, personal communication (lecture at Victoria University of Wellington), 2001.

5   'Overview of NZ in the 19th Century: 1800–40', New Zealand History, https://nzhistory.govt.nz/classroom/ncea3/19th-century-history-overview (accessed September 2019).

6   Ibid.

7   Evelyn Stokes, *Wiremu Tamihana: Rangatira*, Huia, Wellington, 2002, p.218.

8   Jane McRae, 'The Function and Style of Ruunanga in Maori Politics', *Journal of the Polynesian Society*, 93, 4 (1984), pp.283–94.

9   James Belich, *Making Peoples*, Penguin Books, Auckland, 1996; and Paul Diamond, *Savaged to Suit: Māori and Cartooning in New Zealand*, New Zealand Cartoon Archive monograph series, no. 2, Fraser Books, Wellington, 2018.

10 Peter Adds, Brigitte Bönisch-Brednich, Richard S. Hill and Graeme Whimp (eds), *Reconciliation, Representation and Indigeneity: 'Biculturalism' in Aotearoa New Zealand*, Universitätsverlag Winter, Heidelberg, 2016.

11 'Life Expectancy', Ministry of Health Manatū Hauora, 2 August 2018, www.health.govt.nz/our-work/populations/maori-health/tatau-kahukura-maori-health-statistics/nga-mana-hauora-tutohu-health-status-indicators/life-expectancy (accessed 14 January 2020)

12 Moana Jackson, *The Māori and the Criminal Justice System: A New Perspective: He Whaipaanga Hou*, Department of Justice, Wellington, 1988; *Over-Representation of Māori in the Criminal Justice System*, Department of Corrections, Wellington, 2007; *Summary of Our Education for Māori Reports*, Office of the Auditor General, Wellington, 2016, https://www.oag.govt.nz/2016/education-for-maori-summary/docs/summary-education-for-maori.pdf; 'Prison Facts and Statistics – June 2019', Department of Corrections, https://www.corrections.govt.nz/

resources/research_and_statistics/quarterly_prison_statistics/prison_stats_june_2019#ethnicity (accessed 23 October 2019).

13 Letter by Wiremu Tāmihana (my translation), 3 June 1861, *Appendices to the Journal of the House of Representatives* (*AJHR*) 1861, E-1B; 1865, E-11.

14 The figure was $91,000 in 2010: 'Prison Facts and Statistics – June 2010', Department of Corrections, www.corrections.govt.nz/resources/research_and_statistics/quarterly_prison_statistics/previous_years_prison_statistics/march_2011.html (accessed 29 August 2019). It is higher today.

15 Other reference sources consulted for this chapter include: Anton Blank, Carla Houkamau, Carla and Hautahi Kingi, *Unconscious Bias and Education: A Comparative Study of Māori and African American Students*, Oranui Press, Auckland, 2016; E.T. Durie, *Māori Customs and Values in New Zealand Law*, Law Commission: Te Aka Matua o te Ture, Wellington, 2001; C. Knox, 'Whakapūmau te Mauri', PhD thesis, Massey University, 2005; William Colenso, 'Ancient Tide-lore', *Transactions and Proceedings of the Royal Society of New Zealand 1868–1961*, vol. 20, 1887, http://rsnz.natlib.govt.nz/image/rsnz_20/rsnz_20_00_0484_0419_ac_01.html (accessed 29 August 2019) ; and Te Taura Whiri o te Reo Māori, Māori Language Commission, www.tetaurawhiri.govt.nz/about-us/what-is-the-Māori-language-commission/

Chapter 2

1 Graham Hingangaroa Smith and Linda Tuhiwai Smith, 'Doing Indigenous Work: Decolonizing and Transforming the Academy', in E.A. McKinley and L.T. Smith (eds), *Handbook of Indigenous Education*, Springer, Singapore, 2018, pp.1–27.

2 Graham Hingangaroa Smith, 'Kaupapa Maori Theory: Theorizing Indigenous Transformation of Education & Schooling', paper presented at the NZARE/AARE Joint Conference, December 2003, pp.1–17.

3 My thanks to Rebecca Kiddle for providing text, feedback and examples for this chapter, and to Anna Hodge for editorial and structural suggestions.

4   Decolonising work emerges from and acts across many different fields. Authors writing about decolonisation tend to limit themselves just to their field, and decolonising one's own self and practice is a common focus for many (e.g. academics, bloggers). Only a few writers appear to have attempted an overarching theory, and these include Waziyatawin Angela Wilson and Michael Yellow Bird's *For Indigenous Eyes Only: A Decolonization Handbook*, SAR Press, Santa Fe, 2005, and an essay by Pōkā Laenui and Hayden F. Burgess, 'Processes of Decolonization', which can be found in Marie Battiste (ed.), *Reclaiming Indigenous Voice and Vision*, UBC Press, Vancouver, BC, 2000, p.150–59.

5   Brendan Hokowhitu, 'A Genealogy of Indigenous Resistance', in Brendan Hokowhitu, Nathalie Kermoal, Chris Andersen, A. Petersen, Michael P.J. Reilly, Isabel Altamirano-Jimenez and Poia Rewi (eds), *Indigenous Identity and Resistance: Researching the Diversity of Knowledge*, Otago University Press, Dunedin, 2011, p.215.

6   'decolonization', *Oxford English Dictionary*, www.oed.com (accessed 11 December 2019).

7   'decolonisation', *Collins Dictionary and Thesaurus in One Volume*, Collins, London, 1987.

8   'decolonization', Dictionary.com, www.dictionary.com/browse/decolonization (accessed 11 December 2019).

9   'decolonization', *Merriam-Webster Dictionary*, www.merriam-webster.com/dictionary/decolonization (accessed 11 December 2019).

10   Jo Smith, 'Decolonising Dreams and Māori Television', in Jessica Hutchings and Jenny Lee-Morgan (eds), *Decolonisation in Aotearoa: Education, Research and Practice*, NZCER Press, Wellington, 2016, pp.158–71 at p.158.

11   This school of thought, dominant from the 1960s to the 1990s, is often described as postcolonial theory. The term 'postcolonial' is now used less often because of its implication (implicit in the word itself, though not in the theory) that we are in a time *after* colonisation instead of a continuing colonial present.

12   Tracey Banivanua-Mar, *Decolonisation and the Pacific*,

Cambridge University Press, Cambridge, 2016.

13 Lana Lopesi, *False Divides*, Bridget Williams Books, Wellington, 2018.

14 One consequence of the 'false dividing' of the Pacific is that, as Pacific nations, 'we may talk back to the Empire, but we can't talk to each other'. Lopesi, *False Divides*, p.16.

15 Pete George, 'Justice Summit and "Unless We're Willing to Decolonise"', Your NZ, 23 August 2018, https://yournz.org/2018/08/23/justice-summit-and-unless-were-willing-to-decolonise/ (accessed 29 November 2019).

16 Waziyatawin and Yellow Bird, *For Indigenous Eyes Only*, p.4.

17 'decolonise', Urban Dictionary, www.urbandictionary.com/define.php?term=Decolonise

18 In fact, some commentators even suggest that the system enabling Treaty claims actually reinforces colonial power rather than challenging it – see, for instance, Scott Summerfield, 'Towards a Positive Treaty Partnership in the Post-Settlement Era: Treaty of Waitangi Settlements and Decolonisation in Aotearoa New Zealand', MA thesis, Victoria University, Wellington, 2015.

19 Eve Tuck and K. Wayne Yang, 'Decolonization Is Not a Metaphor', *Decolonization: Indigeneity, Education & Society*, 1, 1 (2012), pp.1–40.

20 Rawinia Higgins and Poia Rewi, 'ZePA-Right-shifting: Reorientation towards Normalisation', in Rawinia Higgins, Poia Rewi and Vincent Olsen-Reeder (eds), *The Value of the Māori Language: Te Hua o Te Reo Māori*, Huia, Wellington, 2014, pp.7–32. Some of these actions might include *not* being racist where one's first reaction would be to be.

21 See for example the recent Nike advertising campaign which sought to support African American sportspeople who had suffered the impact of racism, https://thinkprogress.org/nike-kaepernick-campaign-promotes-black-athletes-and-politics/; https://theconversation.com/nikes-courageous-new-ad-campaign-mixing-racial-politics-with-sport-will-be-vindicated-102707

22 Tuck and Yang, 'Decolonization Is Not a Metaphor', p.1.

23 Ngahuia Murphy, 'Menstruation, Whakapapa

and the Revival of Matrilineal Māori Ceremony', in Hutchings and Lee-Morgan (eds), *Decolonisation in Aotearoa*, p.182. Murphy's mention of 'ethnocidal policies' brings to mind the sheer physical damage that an inferiority complex can inflict on colonised peoples – damage which is sheeted home to colonisation only rarely. This damage can manifest itself in a whole spectrum of behaviours, from overachievement and workaholism, to bullying and abuse of others, emotional trauma, experience of poor health due to racism and microaggressions, self-harm and suicide.

24 N.W. Thiong'o, *Decolonising the Mind: The Politics of Language in African Literature*, Heinemann Educational, Portsmouth, 1986.

25 Paulo Freire, *Pedagogy of the Oppressed*, Continuum, New York, 1986, p.133.

26 Waziyatawin and Yellow Bird, *For Indigenous Eyes Only*, p.2.

27 To me that resonates with educational pedagogical literature around the 'threshold' concept. A threshold concept is a cognitive paradigm shift, a point of no return, beyond which a previously difficult to understand idea suddenly fits into place. Like 'taking the red pill' (a reference from the 1999 movie *The Matrix*), it is a realisation that can't be easily undone.

28 Laenui, 'Processes of Decolonization', pp.150–60.

29 Laenui's frames have found resonance with Māori scholars, e.g. Jo Smith, 'Decolonising Dreams and Māori Television', in Hutchings and Lee-Morgan (eds), *Decolonisation in Aotearoa*, pp.158–71 at p.158, borrows from Laenui in her piece on 'dreaming' in the context of Māori TV.

30 Laenui, 'Processes of Decolonization', p.150–52.

31 Soenke Biermann, 'Knowledge, Power and Decolonization: Implications for Non-Indigenous Scholars, Researchers and Educators', in George J. Sefa Dei (ed.), *Indigenous Philosophies and Critical Education: A Reader*, Peter Lang Publishing, New York, 2011, pp.386–98 at p.394.

32 The maramataka suggests lunar phases that are good for fishing and planting.

33 Phrenology is a nineteenth-century pseudoscience

concerning the brain. It supported the idea that some people (such as women and 'tribal' races) generally have innately limited brain capabilities.

34 Laenui, 'Processes of Decolonization', p.152–54. Also described as reawakening by some.

35 Murphy, 'Menstruation, Whakapapa and the Revival of Matrilineal Māori Ceremony', p.182.

36 See Judith Simon and Linda Tuhiwai Smith, *A Civilising Mission? Perceptions and Representations of the New Zealand Native Schools System*, Auckland University Press, Auckland, 2001; J.M. Barrington, *Separate but Equal? Māori Schools and the Crown 1867–1969*, Victoria University Press, Wellington, 2008; Wally Penetito, *What's Māori About Māori Education?*, Victoria University Press, Wellington, 2010.

37 Moana Jackson, 'Decolonising Education', in Hutchings and Lee-Morgan (eds), *Decolonisation in Aotearoa*, p.43.

38 The phrase 'kaupapa Māori' means 'a Māori approach, Māori topic, Māori customary practice, Māori institution, Māori agenda, Māori principles, Māori ideology' (*Te Aka Māori–English, English–Māori Dictionary*, https://maoridictionary.co.nz, accessed 11 December). When capitalised, the phrase refers more specifically to the theory of Kaupapa Māori developed and formalised since the 1970s and now applied in many fields of research and practice.

39 I publish under the name 'Ocean Ripeka Mercier', for instance, to acknowledge my te reo Māori name and identity.

40 Takawai Murphy, 'Decolonising Hearts and Minds in Aotearoa', in Hutchings and Lee-Morgan (eds), *Decolonisation in Aotearoa*, p.85.

41 Laenui, 'Processes of Decolonization', p.155.

42 Cited in Lopesi, *False Divides*, p.92.

43 After the title of the 1990 book by Ranginui Walker, *Ka Whawhai Tonu Mātou: Struggle Without End*, itself drawing on the cry of the defenders of Ōrākau when it was besieged during the New Zealand Wars: 'E hoa, ka whawhai tonu mātou, Āke! Āke! Āke!' (Friend, we will fight on, forever and ever and ever!)

44   Hutchings and Lee-Morgan (eds), *Decolonisation in Aotearoa.*

45   Linda Tuhiwai Smith, *Decolonizing Methodologies: Research and Indigenous Peoples*, 2nd edn, Zed Books, London and New York, 2012. Many Māori researchers would now not consider collaborating with the naïve researcher who wants to work with them but who has not read this book. Thus, and not suprisingly, a large share of decolonisation literature is also around research. Research has strong associations with tertiary education, scholarship and knowledge more generally.

46   International writers inspired by Kaupapa Māori further reference Tuhiwai Smith's book as hugely influential. For example, 'This chapter draws heavily from the work of Māori scholars', US-based Beth Blue Swadener and Kagendo Mutua write in the *Handbook of Critical and Indigenous Methodologies*: 'we draw inspiration but not universal formulas from this powerful body of work.' Beth Blue Swadener and Kagendo Mutua, 'Decolonizing Performances: Deconstructing the Global Postcolonial', in Norman K. Denzin, Yvonna S. Lincoln and Linda Tuhiwai Smith (eds), *Handbook of Critical and Indigenous Methodologies*, Sage Publications, Los Angeles, 2008.

47   From her acceptance speech upon receiving the inaugural Royal Society Te Apārangi Te Puāwaitangi Research Excellence Award. '2018 Te Puāwaitanga Award: Advancing Māori Research, Education and Society', Royal Society Te Apārangi, 17 October 2018, www.royalsociety. org.nz/what-we-do/ medals-and-awards/medals-and-awards-news/2018-te-puawaitanga-award-advancing-maori-research-education-and-society (accessed 14 January 2020).

48   Scotty Morrison, 'Everyone in New Zealand Will Talk Te Reo', Newsroom, 4 September 2019, www.newsroom. co.nz/2019/09/04/785970/ scotty-morrisons-te-reo-revolution-the-latest-chapter# (accessed 7 January 2020).

49   Smith, *Decolonizing Methodologies*, p.4.

50   Ngā mihi nui to my co-author

Rebecca for providing the text and examples in these two paragraphs.

51 See for example Ngāti Whātua Ōrākei's medium-density housing development: www.aucklanddesignmanual.co.nz/design-subjects/maori-design/papakaingahousing resource/guidance/success-stories/kainga-tuatahi

52 At the time of writing, the borrowing cap for loans for building houses on collectively owned land is just $200,000. (See here for more information on the difficulties of building on Māori collectively owned land: https://ngatiporou.com/article/living-east-coast-dream.) In 2018, the average cost per square metre of building a house was $2,513 for a low-rise house in Wellington and $2,700 in Auckland (www2.deloitte.com/content/dam/Deloitte/nz/Documents/Economics/nz-en-DAE-Fletcher-cost-of-residential-housing-development.pdf, p. 60). Houses built using the only funding mechanism available to borrow money on Māori-owned land must be low rise; in fact, they must be built on piles so that, if the mortgagee defaults on their payments, the house can be cut from its piles, put on a truck and taken away. A two-bedroom house might typically be 100 square metres in size, so building a two-bedroom house in Wellington might cost approximately $251,300 – well above the borrowing cap. Even for a small house, funding would be a struggle – not to mention the funding required to build a larger home where Māori whānau can live in extended family groupings.

53 For example the signs made by rangatahi in Bianca's Te Puna Mātauranga in Takapūwāhia (https://poriruacity.govt.nz/your-council/news/celebrating-m%C4%81ori-language-day-bilingual-signs/), or the haka lanterns developed by Wellington City Council for Te Matatini, the kapa haka competition (www.stuff.co.nz/dominion-post/capital-life/capital-day/110723741/crossing-light-change-all-go-during-te-matatini).

54 Waziyatawin and Yellow Bird, *For Indigenous Eyes Only*, p.2.

55 Malcolm X, 'Who Taught You to Hate?' speech excerpt, Educational Video Group, Greenwood, 5 May 1962,

https://video.alexanderstreet.com/watch/malcolm-x-who-taught-you-to-hate-speech-excerpt (accessed 7 January 2020).

56 Wanda D. McCaslin and Denise C. Breton, 'Justice as Healing: Going Outside the Colonizers' Cage', in Denzin, Lincoln and Smith (eds), *Handbook of Critical and Indigenous Methodologies*, p.515.

57 Murphy, 'Decolonising Hearts and Minds in Aotearoa', p.84.

58 For instance, Devon A. Mihesuah and Angela Cavender Wilson (eds), *Indigenizing the Academy: Transforming Scholarship and Empowering Communities*, University of Nebraska Press, Lincoln, 2004.

59 Smith, 'Kaupapa Maori Theory'; Hokowhitu, 'A Genealogy of Indigenous Resistance'.

60 Puawai Cairns, 'Decolonisation: We Aren't Going to Save You', Center for the Future of Museums blog, American Alliance of Museums, 17 December 2018, www.aam-us.org/2018/12/17/decolonisation-we-arent-going-to-save-you/ (accessed 11 November 2019).

61 McCaslin and Breton, 'Justice as Healing', p.512.

62 Laenui, 'Processes of Decolonization', p.151.

63 Jo Moir, 'Parents at Centre of Oranga Tamariki Child Uplift Won't Take Part in Government Review', RNZ, 29 October 2019, www.rnz.co.nz/news/political/401978/parents-at-centre-of-oranga-tamariki-child-uplift-won-t-take-part-in-government-review (accessed 29 November 2019).

64 Laenui, 'Processes of Decolonization', p.151.

65 Such as Leanne R. Simpson, 'Anticolonial Strategies for the Recovery and Maintenance of Indigenous Knowledge', *American Indian Quarterly*, 28, 3 & 4 (2004), pp.373–84, and Deborah McGregor, 'The State of Traditional Ecological Knowledge Research in Canada: A Critique of Current Theory and Practice', in Ron F. Laliberte et al. (eds), *Expressions in Canadian Native Studies*, University Extension Press, Saskatoon, 2000.

66 Leanne R. Simpson further recounts being asked to 'depoliticise' her journal submissions, because decolonising narratives are supposedly irrelevant to

science – a story that smacks of political and intellectual colonialism. Simpson, 'Anticolonial Strategies for the Recovery and Maintenance of Indigenous Knowledge', pp.373–84.

67 Laenui, 'Processes of Decolonization', p.152.

68 Cairns, 'Decolonisation'.

69 Ibid.

70 Jackson, 'Decolonising Education', p.46.

71 Jane Kelsey, *No Ordinary Deal: Unmasking the Trans-Pacific Partnership Free Trade Agreement*, Bridget Williams Books, Wellington, 2010.

72 See Maria Bargh, 'A Blue Economy for Aotearoa New Zealand?', *Environment, Development and Sustainability*, 16, 3 (2014), pp.459–70.

73 Jackson, 'Decolonising Education', p.47.

74 Tuck and Yang, 'Decolonization Is Not a Metaphor'.

75 Smith, 'Kaupapa Maori Theory', p.2.

76 Brendan Hokowhitu, 'Indigenous Existentialism and the Body', *Cultural Studies Review*, 15, 2 (2009), pp.101–18 at pp.104–5.

77 Pamela Palmater, 'Decolonization Is Taking Back Our Power', in Peter McFarlane and Nicole Schabus (eds), *Whose Land Is It Anyway? A Manual for Decolonization*, Federation of Post-Secondary Educators of BC, British Columbia, 2017, pp.73–78.

78 Smith, 'Kaupapa Maori Theory'.

79 Hokowhitu, 'Indigenous Existentialism and the Body', pp.101–2.

Chapter 3

1 We suggest even new migrants benefit from systems that support those who have similar values and worldviews and/or who look and act as Pākehā.

2 Ngā mihi to Rachel Kingi, Rachel Marwick, Jessica Sewell, Elisapeta Heta, Maxine Boag and Tina Ngata for their contributions to this chapter. I appreciate their tautoko and the whakaaro that has helped frame this chapter.

3 Awanui Te Huia and James H. Liu, 'Māori Culture as a Psychological Asset for New Zealanders' Acculturation Experiences Abroad', *International Journal of Intercultural Relations*, 36, 1 (2012), pp.140–50 at p.141.

4 While I have Pākehā heritage

as well as Māori, to aid clarity of expression I use the pronouns 'they'/'them' when talking about Pākehā.

5   Rachel Kingi, personal communication, 2017.

6   Glenn Colquhoun (2015), 'The Last Pākehā', in Heather Came and Amy Zander (eds), *State of the Pākehā Nation: Collected Waitangi Day Speeches and Essays, 2006–2015*, Network Waitangi Whangarei, Whāngārei, 2015, p.56, https://trc.org.nz/sites/trc.org.nz/files/digital%20library/State%20of%20the%20P%C4%81keh%C4%81%20Nation.pdf (accessed 21 November 2019).

7   Ibid.

8   Te Huia and Liu, 'Māori Culture as a Psychological Asset for New Zealanders' Acculturation Experiences Abroad', p.141.

9   Colquhoun, 'The Last Pākehā', pp.53–54.

10 Rachel Marwick, personal communication, 2017.

11 Catherine Delahunty, 'Flush and Forget – Pākehā and Te Tiriti', in Came and Zander (eds), *State of the Pākehā Nation*.

12 Olga Khazan, 'Inherited Trauma Shapes Your Health', *The Atlantic*, 16 October 2018, www.theatlantic.com/health/archive/2018/10/trauma-inherited-generations/573055/ (accessed 23 October 2019).

13 Jessica Sewell, personal communication, 2017.

14 Avril Bell, 'Decolonizing Conviviality and "Becoming Ordinary": Cross-Cultural Face-to-Face Encounters in Aotearoa New Zealand', *Ethnic and Racial Studies*, 39, 7 (2016), pp.1170–86 at 1173–74.

15 Jo Smith, 'Aotearoa/New Zealand: An Unsettled State in a Sea of Islands', *Settler Colonial Studies*, 1, 1 (2011), pp.111–31 at p.112.

16 Ibid., p.128.

17 Te Huia and Liu, 'Māori Culture as a Psychological Asset for New Zealanders' Acculturation Experiences Abroad', pp.140–50.

18 Stella Ting-Toomey, 'Identity Negotiation Theory: Cross Cultural Boundaries', in William B. Gudykunst (ed.), *Theorizing about Intercultural Communication*, Sage Publishing, Thousand Oaks, California, 2005.

19 Colquhoun, 'The Last Pākehā', p.54.

20 Elisapeta Heta, personal communication, 2017.

21 Kassie Hartendorp, 'Utu

and Capitalism: A Harmful Imbalance', *Continuum*, 32, 6 (2018), pp.678–84.

22 See, for example, the famous Ngāti Toa case whereby iwi gave the Anglican Church land in Porirua to build a school. Despite the fact that it was never built, the Crown later declared that the church owned the land. When Wi Parata took the case to court, Chief Justice James Prendergast's decision was that the courts lacked the ability to consider claims based on native title and the Treaty of Waitangi was 'worthless', and a 'simple nullity'. This decision would later be used to justify the continued alienation of Māori land. 'Chief Justice Declares Treaty "Worthless" and a "Simple Nullity"', New Zealand History, https://nzhistory.govt.nz/ the-chief-justice-declares-that-the-treaty-of-waitangi-is-worthless-and-a-simple-nullity (accessed 23 October 2019).

23 Gareth Morgan, 'Why We Need to Shift to Capital Taxes', in *The Piketty Phenomenon: New Zealand Perspectives*, Bridget Williams Books, Wellington, 2014, p.112.

24 See, for example, Allister Heath, 'Thomas Piketty's Bestselling Post-Crisis Manifesto is Horrendously Flawed', *Telegraph*, 29 April 2014, www.telegraph.co.uk/ finance/economics/10796532/ Thomas-Pikettys-bestselling-post-crisis-manifesto-is-horrendously-flawed.html (accessed 23 October 2019); or Chris Giles, 'Piketty Findings Undercut by Errors', *Financial Times*, 23 May 2014, www. ft.com/content/e1f343ca-e281-11e3-89fd-00144feabdc0 (accessed 23 October 2019).

25 See Helen Moewaka Barnes, E. Eich and S. Yessilth, 'Colonization, Whenua and Capitalism: Experiences from Aotearoa New Zealand', *Continuum*, 32, 6 (2018), pp.685–97, for an account of the interrelationship between colonisation, capitalism and land.

26 David Callahan, 'The Biggest Problem With Capitalism That Nobody Talks About', *Dēmos*, 31 January 2014, www.demos. org/blog/biggest-problem-capitalism-nobody-talks-about (accessed 23 October 2019).

27 Rupert Neate, 'Richest 1% Own Half the World's Wealth, Study Finds', *Guardian*, 14 November

2017, www.theguardian.com/inequality/2017/nov/14/worlds-richest-wealth-credit-suisse (accessed 23 October 2019).

28 Callahan, 'The Biggest Problem With Capitalism That Nobody Talks About'.

29 Maxine Boag, personal communication, 2017.

30 Max Rashbrooke, *Wealth and New Zealand*, Bridget Williams Books, Wellington, 2015, p.215.

31 Ibid., p.218.

32 Andy Fyers, 'The Truth about Inequality in New Zealand', Stuff Business, 17 January 2017, www.stuff.co.nz/business/88455171/the-truth-about-inequality-in-new-zealand (accessed 23 October 2019). See Max Rashbrooke, *The Inequality Debate*, Bridget Williams Books, Wellington, 2014, for a fuller discussion on this.

33 Lisa Marriott and Dalice Sim, *Indicators of Inequality for Māori and Pacific People*, Working Paper 09/2014, Papers in Public Finance, Victoria University of Wellington, August 2014, www.victoria.ac.nz/sacl/centres-and-chairs/cpf/publications/working-papers/WP09_2014_Indicators-of-Inequality.pdf (accessed 21 November 2019).

34 Rashbrooke, *Wealth and New Zealand*, p.69.

35 Ibid., p.20.

36 Alan Johnson, Philippa Howden-Chapman and Shamubeel Eaqub, *A Stocktake of New Zealand's Housing, February 2018*, Ministry of Business, Innovation and Employment, Wellington, 2018, www.beehive.govt.nz/sites/default/files/2018-02/A%20Stocktake%20Of%20New%20Zealand%27s%20Housing.pdf (accessed 21 November 2019).

37 Ibid.

38 Rashbrooke, *Wealth and New Zealand*, p.20.

39 Joshua Hitchcock, 'The $50 Billion Māori Economy Is Nowhere Big Enough', The Spinoff, 5 March 2019, https://thespinoff.co.nz/atea/05-03-2019/the-50-billion-maori-economy-is-nowhere-big-enough/ (accessed 23 October 2019).

40 Tom Carver and Arthur Grimes, *Income or Consumption: Which Better Predicts Subjective Wellbeing?*, Motu Working Paper 16-12, Motu Economic and Public Policy Research, August 2016, executive summary, https://motu.nz/assets/Documents/our-work/wellbeing-and-

macroeconomics/well-being-and-sustainability-measures/Income-or-Consumption-Exec-Summary.pdf (accessed 21 November 2019).

41 Pascarn Dickenson, 'The Sensitivity of Wellbeing to Inequalities in Local Wellbeing', MA thesis, Victoria University, Wellington, 2018.

42 Tina Ngata, personal communication, 2017.

43 Steven Davey, Anaru Waa, Sarah Gordon, Ramona Tiatia and Toa Waaka, 'Mental Distress, Stigma and Social Exclusion in Aotearoa/New Zealand: Māori Solutions to a Pākehā Problem', 2019, manuscript submitted for publication.

44 Noam Chomsky quoted in Alexandra Rosenmann, 'Chomsky: America Is on the Decline: Guess Who's to Blame?', AlterNet, 15 July 2016, www.alternet.org/2016/07/chomsky-america-decline-guess-whos-blame/ (accessed 23 October 2019).

45 Max Harris, 'Racism and White Defensiveness in Aotearoa: A Pākehā Perspective', E-Tangata, 10 June 2018, https://e-tangata.co.nz/comment-and-analysis/racism-and-white-defensiveness-in-aotearoa-a-pakeha-perspective/ (accessed 23 October 2019).

Chapter 4

1 Laura Pulido, 'Geographies of Race and Ethnicity 1: White Supremacy vs White Privilege in Environmental Racism Research', Progress in Human Geography, 39, 6 (2015), pp.809–17; see also Eleanor Brittain, 'Whai Tikanga: In Pursuit of Justice: Māori Interactions with the Criminal Justice System and Experiences of Institutional Racism', MA thesis, Massey University, 2016.

2 Avril Bell, 'Bifurcation or Entanglement? Settler Identity and Biculturalism in Aotearoa New Zealand', Continuum, 20, 2 (2006), pp.253–68; Ani Mikaere, Colonising Myths – Māori Realities: He Rukuruku Whakaaro, Huia: Te Tākupu, Te Wānanga o Raukawa, Wellington, 2011.

3 Waitangi Tribunal, The Ngāi Tahu Land Report 1991, https://forms.justice.govt.nz/search/Documents/WT/wt_DOC_68476209/Wai27.pdf (accessed 26 November 2018).

4 Bell, 'Bifurcation or Entanglement?'

5 Diana Amundsen,

'Decolonisation through Reconciliation: The Role of Pākehā Identity', *MAI Journal*, 7, 2 (2018), pp.139–54; Rachael Fabish, 'Black Rainbow: Stories of Māori and Pākehā Working across Difference', PhD thesis, Victoria University, Wellington, 2014.

6   Max Harris, 'Racism and White Defensiveness in Aotearoa: A Pākehā Perspective', *E-Tangata*, 10 June 2018, https://e-tangata. co.nz/comment-and-analysis/racism-and-white-defensiveness-in-aotearoa-a-pakeha-perspective/ (accessed 8 October 2018).

7   Eve Tuck and K. Wayne Yang, 'Decolonization Is Not a Metaphor', *Decolonization: Indigeneity, Education & Society*, 1, 1 (2012), pp.1–40.

8   Graham Smith, interviewed by Te Kawehau Hoskins and Alison Jones, 'Interview: Kaupapa Māori: The Dangers of Domestication', *New Zealand Journal of Educational Studies*, 47, 2 (2012), pp.10–20.

9   Episode 5 of the podcast *Taringa*, produced by Te Wānanga o Aotearoa, has a really great discussion of the importance of pronouncing the long vowel sounds that macrons denote.

10 Kirsty Johnston, 'How NZ Police Use Tactical Options', *New Zealand Herald*, 23 March 2017, https://insights. nzherald.co.nz/article/police-tactical-options/ (accessed 4 October 2019).

11 Pania Te Whaiti and Michael Roguski, *Māori Perceptions of the Police*, He Pārekereke/Victoria Link Ltd, September 1998, www. police.govt.nz/sites/default/ files/publications/maori-perceptions-of-police.pdf (accessed 2 October 2019).

12 Ibid., p.30.

13 Vine Deloria, Jr, *Custer Died for Your Sins: An Indian Manifesto*, University of Oklahoma Press, Norman, Oklahoma, 1988, p.4.

14 Leonie Pihama interviewed by Dale Husband, 'Let's Start by Returning the Waitara Land', *E-Tangata*, 1 July 2018, https:// e-tangata.co.nz/korero/ leonie-pihama-lets-start-by-returning-the-waitara-land/ (accessed 9 November 2018).

15 Linda Tuhiwai Smith, *Decolonizing Methodologies: Research and Indigenous Peoples*, Zed Books, London, 1999.

16 Jen Margaret, *Working as Allies: Supporters of Indigenous Justice Reflect,*

Auckland Workers' Educational Association, Auckland, 2013.

17   Tuck and Yang, 'Decolonization Is Not a Metaphor', p.19.

18   Pihama, interviewed by Husband, 'Let's Start by Returning the Waitara Land'.

19   See www.protectihumatao.com

20   Andy Fyers, 'The Amount Allocated to Treaty of Waitangi Settlements is Tiny, Compared with Other Government Spending', Stuff, 3 August 2018, www.stuff.co.nz/national/104205997/the-amount-allocated-to-treaty-settlements-is-tiny-compared-with-other-government-spending (accessed 14 January 2020)

21   Courtney Ariel, 'For Our White Friends Desiring to Be Allies', *Sojourners*, 16 August 2017, https://sojo.net/articles/our-white-friends-desiring-be-allies?fbclid=IwAR1D3VO2aTjY0oCndxyvtDiZKgOq_Z8aFKlJF8uPVXV4PCZhcSa-L0dzbBc (accessed 26 November 2018).

22   'Some Māori Are Struggling with "Language Trauma" as Number of Kiwis Learning Te Reo Continues to Surge, Scotty Morrison Says', One News Now, 31 July 2018, www.tvnz.co.nz/one-news/new-zealand/some-m-ori-struggling-language-trauma-number-kiwis-learning-te-reo-continues-surge-scotty-morrison-says (accessed 1 August 2018).

23   Mikaere, *Colonising Myths – Māori Realities.*

24   Frances Lee, 'Why I've Started to Fear My Fellow Social Justice Activists', *Yes!* 13 October 2017, www.yesmagazine.org/people-power/why-ive-started-to-fear-my-fellow-social-justice-activists-20171013 (accessed 29 October 2018).

25   Alexis Shotwell, 'A Politics of Imperfection, A Politics of Responsibility', 25 April 2017, https://alexisshotwell.com/2017/04/25/a-politics-of-imperfection-a-politics-of-responsibility/ (accessed 29 October 2018).

26   Margaret, *Working as Allies.*

27   If you want more inspiration for responses, a group called Kupu Taea came up with a booklet with some great responses to anti-Māori themes in news media. You can find it here: https://trc.org.nz/alternatives-anti-Māori-themes-news-media

28 Judith Simon and Linda Tuhiwai Smith, *A Civilising Mission? Perceptions and Representations of the Native School System*, Auckland University Press, Auckland, 2001.

29 JustSpeak, *The Case against Prisons: A JustSpeak Report*, Wellington, 2018.

30 Diana Amundsen, 'Decolonisation through Reconciliation: The Role of Pākehā Identity', *MAI Journal*, 7, 2 (2018), pp.139–54.

Chapter 5

1 The 'blue water' doctrine, principle or thesis, also known as the 'Salt Water Thesis' or the 'Belgian Thesis', is an idea arising out of a UN Resolution (637) which suggested that to be eligible for decolonisation a body of water or a discrete geographical boundary of some sort was needed between the colonising country and the colony. The United States argued that it, and other countries like New Zealand, Australia and Canada, shouldn't need to give Indigenous peoples in these countries the right to self-determination as 'colonialism requires sea-based conquest' (Robbins, 2015). See Bruce Robbins,

'Blue Water: A Thesis', *Review of International American Studies*, 8, 1 (2015), pp.47–66.

2 Rarawa Kohere, personal communication.

3 Jean Riki, 'Te Wā Kāinga – Home', in Paula Abood, Barry Gamba and Michelle Kotevski (eds), *Waiting in Space: An Anthology of Australian Writing*, Pluto Press, Annandale NSW, 1999.

4 Patricia Grace, *Potiki*, Penguin Books, 1986, p.39.

5 Arapera Kaa Blank, *Ngā Kōkako Huataratara: The Notched Plumes of the Kōkako*, The Waiata Koa Trust, 1986, p.64.

6 Ani Mikaere, *Colonising Myths – Māori Realities: He Rukuruku Whakaaro*, Huia: Te Tākupu, Te Wānanga o Raukawa, Wellington, 2011, p.208.

7 Moana Maniapoto, 'Ancestors', on Moana and the Moahunters, *Rua*, Tangata Records, 1998.

8 Rudyard Kipling, 'The White Man's Burden: The United States and the Philippine Islands', in *Rudyard Kipling's Verse: Definitive Edition*, Hodder and Stoughton, London, 1940, pp.323–24, as found at RPO: Representative Poems Online,

University of Toronto Library, https://rpo.library.utoronto.ca/poems/white-mans-burden (accessed 13 November 2019).

9 Elsdon Best, *Māori Religion and Mythology: Being an Account of the Cosmogony, Anthropogeny, Religious Beliefs and Rites, Magic and Folk Lore of the Maori Folk of New Zealand, Part 1*, A.R. Shearer, Government Printer, Wellington, 1976, p.31.

10 *He Whakaaro Here Whakaumu Mō Aotearoa: The Report of Matike Mai Aotearoa – The Independent Working Group on Constitutional Transformation*, Matike Mai Aotearoa, 2016, p.69, www.converge.org.nz/pma/MatikeMaiAotearoaReport.pdf (accessed 9 December 2019).

11 Philip McKibbin, *Love Notes: For a Politics of Love*, Lantern Books, New York, 2019, p.ix.

12 Thomas King, *The Truth about Stories: A Native Narrative*, CBC Massey Lectures, House of Anansi Press, Dead Dog Café Productions and Canadian Broadcasting Corporation, 2003, p.2.

13 Ben Okri, *A Way of Being Free*, Phoenix House, London, 1997, p.112.

14 Allen Curnow, 'The Skeleton of the Great Moa in Canterbury Museum, Christchurch', in Ian Wedde and Harvey McQueen (eds), *The Penguin Book of New Zealand Verse*, Penguin Books, Auckland, 1985, p.199.

15 Witi Ihimaera, 'Our Watch Now', in Reina Whaitiri and Robert Sullivan (eds), *Puna Wai Kōrero: An Anthology of Māori Poetry in English*, Auckland University Press, Auckland, 2014, p.118.

ACKNOWLEDGEMENTS

He murimuri aroha nōku ki a Tāne whakapiripiri
Ka ori i te whare
Kei te haruru tonu taku puku
Tō rekareka kei tuku atu
Ki te anu o te tonga

I look with deep affection
at an agitated house
My heart is unsettled
lest our joy be resigned
to the cold.

Ngā mihi to Ngāti Toa Rangatira for allowing us to undertake the Imagining Decolonised Cities (IDC) project in their rohe. Ngā mihi to the New Zealand National Commission for UNESCO and Te Herenga Waka – Victoria University of Wellington for funding the original IDC project. For more information on the project that sparked the idea for this book, please go to www.idcities.co.nz.

Ngā mihi to Bridget Williams Books and in particular Tom Rennie, Laura Koziol and Anna Hodge for their editorial support and willingness to produce this book.

Ngā mihi to all of those who have resisted colonisation and its ongoing impacts on Māori whānau and fought for an Aotearoa that cherishes te ao Māori, whether that be in very public acts of protest or in private and everyday acts of resistance. We are grateful for your painstaking, tireless and ongoing mahi. We are hopeful that this book builds on your work. We are hopeful that New Zealanders will not only imagine a decolonised Aotearoa New Zealand but work to create a country that is truly based on Te Tiriti and the relationships it envisaged.

ABOUT THE AUTHORS

Bianca Elkington
Bianca is Ngāti Toa Rangatira. She is the Iwi Education Coordinator at Te Rūnanga o Toa Rangatira Incorporated and leads the innovative marae-based education programme, Te Puna Mātauranga at Takapūwāhia, Porirua. This programme supports Māori education through a unique model of collaboration between iwi, schools and whānau. She's passionate about seeing Māori tamariki and rangatahi succeed.

Moana Jackson
Moana Jackson is Ngāti Kahungunu, Ngāti Porou and Rongomaiwahine. Moana likes telling stories to and for his mokopuna and hopes they will grow up in a land where Te Tiriti is finally seen as the base for respectful political relationships. Then there will be other stories to tell.

Rebecca Kiddle
Becky is Ngāti Porou and Ngāpuhi and grew up in Havelock North, a predominantly Pākehā community in Kahungunu territory. She was sent to St Joseph's Māori Girls College to learn about her Māoritanga. She is still on this journey and, while her learning journey is more of a plod, she

continues to hope for more reo and tikanga fluency, to learn more mātauranga Māori and ultimately to see social and cultural justice for Māori whānau.

Ocean Ripeka Mercier

Ocean is of Ngāti Porou and Cornish descent. She was raised in the suburb of Northland, Te Whang-anui-a-Tara/Wellington. Like many residents of the area she grew up knowing Te Ahumairangi, the local maunga, as 'Tinnakoory Hill'. Ocean studied and worked at the university variously known as Victoria College and Te Whare Wānanga o te Ūpoko o te Ika a Māui. Places and landscapes have been renamed all around her and she loves nothing better than to think and run in amongst it all, sometimes with a map in hand.

Michael Ross

Tainui te waka, Ngāti Hauā te iwi, Kai-a-te-mata te marae.

Mike grew up in a blue collar whānau in Porirua, with frequent trips and stays amongst his extended Hotene whānau. He's always loved everything about being Māori: the sounds, the food, the look, the people, and the ways. This led to roles supporting Māori in communities and eventually to teaching in Te Kawa a Māui at Te Herenga Waka – Victoria University Wellington.

Jennie Smeaton

Jennie is Ngāti Toa Rangatira. Her background is in environmental management and policy development. She has held roles working for her iwi in an environmental management capacity and supporting the negotiation of the Ngāti Toa Rangatira Treaty of Waitangi claim. She is currently a Principal Advisor at Te Puni Kōkiri, the Ministry of Māori Development. She truly believes that te ao Māori is beneficial for not only our people but for all.

Amanda Thomas

Amanda is from Horomaka/Banks Peninsula and Ōtautahi/Christchurch, and now lives in Pōneke/Wellington. She grew up surrounded by stories about Ngāi Tahu but didn't do much thinking about what it meant to be Pākehā in Ngāi Tahu territory until recently. Now she thinks about Pākehā-ness a lot, what it means and how to have good relationships with Māori and Aotearoa New Zealand. Her friends and family are probably quite sick of being sounding boards but are generous about it all the same.

About BWB Texts

BWB Texts are short books on big subjects from great New Zealand writers. They are succinct narratives spanning contemporary issues, memoir, history and science. With well over fifty BWB Texts in print and more available digitally, new works are published regularly. BWB Texts can be purchased from all good bookstores and online from www.bwb.co.nz.

BWB Texts include:

Transforming the Welfare State: Towards a New Social Contract
Jonathan Boston

#NoFly
Shaun Hendy

Rebuilding the Kāinga: Lessons from Te Ao Hurihuri
Jade Kake

The Broken Estate: Journalism and Democracy in a Post-Truth World
Mel Bunce

Student Political Action in New Zealand
Sylvia Nissen

A Careful Revolution: Towards a Low-Emissions Future
David Hall

The Health of the People
David Skegg

Still Counting
Marilyn Waring

Maui Street
Morgan Godfery

Mountains to Sea
Mike Joy (ed.)

Ko Taranaki Te Maunga
Rachel Buchanan

False Divides
Lana Lopesi

A Matter of Fact: Talking Truth in a Post-Truth World
Jess Berentson-Shaw

Better Lives: Migration, Wellbeing and New Zealand
Julie Fry and Peter Wilson

Doing Our Bit: The Campaign to Double the Refugee Quota
Murdoch Stephens

The Stolen Island: Searching for 'Ata
Scott Hamilton

The Post-Snowden Era: Mass Surveillance and Privacy in New Zealand
Kathleen Kuehn

The Bike and Beyond: Life on Two Wheels in Aotearoa New Zealand
Laura Williamson

Late Love: Sometimes Doctors Need Saving as Much as Their Patients
Glenn Colquhoun

Three Cities: Seeking Hope in the Anthropocene
Rod Oram

Playing for Both Sides: Love Across the Tasman
Stephanie Johnson

Complacent Nation
Gavin Ellis

The First Migration: Māori Origins 3000BC – AD1450
Atholl Anderson

Silencing Science
Shaun Hendy

Going Places: Migration, Economics and the Future of New Zealand
Julie Fry and Hayden Glass

The Interregnum: Rethinking New Zealand
Morgan Godfery (ed.)

Christchurch Ruptures
Katie Pickles

Home Truths: Confronting New Zealand's Housing Crisis
Philippa Howden-Chapman

Polluted Inheritance: New Zealand's Freshwater Crisis
Mike Joy

Wealth and New Zealand
Max Rashbrooke